Online Social Networks

Online Social Networks

Laurie Collier Hillstrom

LUCENT BOOKS
A part of Gale, Cengage Learning

GALE
CENGAGE Learning

Detroit • New York • San Francisco • New Haven, Conn • Waterville, Maine • London

GALE
CENGAGE Learning™

LIBRARY OF CONGRESS CATALOGING-IN-PUBLICATION DATA

Hillstrom, Laurie Collier, 1965-
    Online social networks / by Laurie Collier Hillstrom.
        p. cm. — (Technology 360)
    Includes bibliographical references and index.
    ISBN 978-1-4205-0167-4 (hardcover)
   1. Online social networks. I. Title.
    HM742.H55 2010
    302.30285—dc22
    2009045044

Lucent Books
27500 Drake Rd
Farmington Hills MI 48331

ISBN-13: 978-1-4205-0167-4
ISBN-10: 1-4205-0167-4

Printed in the United States of America
1 2 3 4 5 6 7 14 13 12 11 10

Printed by Bang Printing, Brainerd, MN, 1st Ptg., 04/2010

CONTENTS

FOREWORD

"As we go forward, I hope we're going to continue to use technology to make really big differences in how people live and work."
—Sergey Brin, co-founder of Google

The past few decades have seen some amazing advances in technology. Many of these changes have had a direct and measurable impact on the way people live, work, and play. Communication tools, such as cell phones, satellites, and the Internet, allow people to keep in constant contact across longer distances and from the most remote places. In fields related to medicine, existing technologies— digital imaging devices, robotics, and lasers, for example— are being used to redefine surgical procedures and diagnostic techniques. As technology has becomes more complex, however, so have the related ethical, legal, and safety issues.

Psychologist B.F. Skinner once noted that "the real problem is not whether machines think but whether men do." Recent advances in technology have, in many cases, drastically changed the way people view the world around them. They can have a conversation with someone across the globe at lightening speed, access a huge universe of information with the click of a key, or become an avatar in a virtual world of their own making. While advances like these have been viewed as a great boon in some quarters, they have also opened the door to questions about whether or not the speed of technological advancement has come at an unspoken price. A closer examination of the evolution and use of these devices provides a deeper understanding of the social, cultural, and ethical implications that they may hold for our future.

Technology 360 not only explores how evolving technologies work, but also examines the short- and long-term impact of their use on society as a whole. Each volume in Technology 360 focuses on a particular invention, device, or family of similar devices, exploring how the device was developed; how it works; its impact on society; and possible future uses. Volumes also contain a chronology specific to each topic, a glossary of technical terms used in the text, and a subject index. Sidebars, photos and detailed illustrations, tables, charts, and graphs help further illuminate the text.

Titles in this series emphasize inventions and devices familiar to most readers, such as robotics, digital cameras, iPods, and video games. Not only will users get an easy-to-understand, "nuts and bolts" overview of these inventions, they will also learn just how much these devices have evolved. For example, in 1973 a Motorola cell phone weighed about 2 pounds (0.907kg) and cost $4000.00—today, cell phones weigh only a few ounces and are inexpensive enough for every member of the family to have one. Lasers—long a staple of the industrial world—have become highly effective surgical tools, capable of reshaping the cornea of the eye and cleaning clogged arteries. Early video games were played on large machines in arcades; now, many families play games on sophisticated home systems that allow for multiple players and cross-location networking.

IMPORTANT DATES

1971
Computer engineer Ray Tomlinson invents e-mail.

1981
IBM introduces the first personal computer, or PC.

1979
USENET newsgroups are among the first online communities.

1985
Artists, writers, philosophers, scientists, and other intellectuals exchange views and express opinions on an influential online community called the WELL.

1993
Marc Andreessen introduces the Mosaic Web browser, which soon becomes Netscape.

1970   1980   1990

1969
Researchers at the U.S. Department of Defense create the ARPANET.

1991
Tim Berners-Lee invents the World Wide Web.

1997
The term *weblog* is first used to describe online journals or diaries. One of the earliest social networking sites, SixDegrees.com, appears online.

in the Development of Online Social Networks

2002
Internet entrepreneur Jonathan Abrams launches Friendster.

2003
Several new social networking sites appear, including MySpace and LinkedIn.

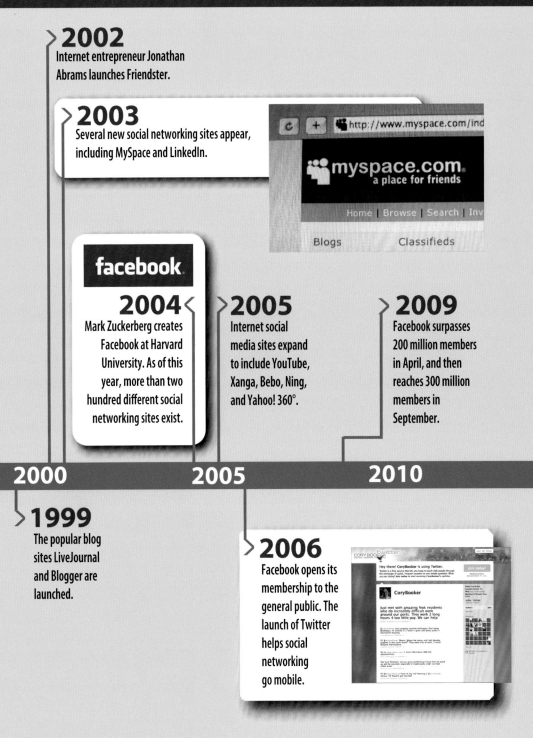

2004
Mark Zuckerberg creates Facebook at Harvard University. As of this year, more than two hundred different social networking sites exist.

2005
Internet social media sites expand to include YouTube, Xanga, Bebo, Ning, and Yahoo! 360°.

2009
Facebook surpasses 200 million members in April, and then reaches 300 million members in September.

2000

2005

2010

1999
The popular blog sites LiveJournal and Blogger are launched.

2006
Facebook opens its membership to the general public. The launch of Twitter helps social networking go mobile.

Connecting Online

Human beings have formed social networks through-out history. Belonging to groups made it easier for people to communicate, exchange information, provide support, solve problems, and work cooperatively to achieve goals. Traditional social networks generally consist of people within a limited geographical area, such as members of a family, residents of a town or neighborhood, students at a school, members of a church, or employees of a company.

Around the turn of the twenty-first century, however, the age-old concept of social networks underwent a dramatic change. As Internet access expanded throughout the world and grew faster and more reliable, new technologies appeared to help people communicate, share information, and build communities online. These technologies, which became known as online social networks, have revolutionized the way that people connect, interact, and form relationships. "It has opened up new networks where far-away strangers can become close friends, where families and friends can share common experiences though far apart, and where colleagues can work on teams with people they've never seen,"[1] Mike Reid and Christian Gray explain in an article for *Internet Librarian*.

By 2009 there were hundreds of different social networking sites on the Internet. Some of the most popular

Online social networks have allowed people around the world to interact in new and exciting ways.

and influential sites in North America include Facebook, MySpace, Twitter, LinkedIn, and Bebo. The various online social networks target different demographic groups, use different technological platforms, offer different applications and features, and offer their own distinct culture. Yet all of the sites are alike in that they provide online environments in which members can build a personal profile, establish connections with other members, exchange messages, and share digital content, such as photos, videos, and music.

Altogether, online social networks have helped 100 million Americans and half a billion people around the world interact with each other in fascinating new ways. "Social networking, when used appropriately, can hold great promise," online service provider TDS Telecommunications Corp. notes. "It brings friends and families together, expands one's knowledge base, exposes people to new and interesting things and, in some instances, can lead to new professional and personal opportunities."[2]

CHAPTER 1

The Internet and Early Online Communities

S ocial interaction has been an important function of the Internet ever since the technology was first developed in the 1960s. In fact, the main idea behind the creation of the Internet was to make it easier for people to communicate by linking their computers together electronically. As Internet technology improved over time, methods of socializing online grew more sophisticated as well.

Birth of the Internet

Online social networking would not be possible without the Internet, the vast system of interconnected computer networks that stretches around the world. The earliest ancestor of the modern Internet was a computer network called the ARPANET. It was created in 1969 by a group of scientists and engineers who worked for the Advanced Research Projects Agency (ARPA) in the U.S. Department of Defense. They originally wanted to build an electronic communication system that could carry military data without interruption.

BITS & BYTES

8

Number of social networks among the twenty largest Web sites in the world as of 2009

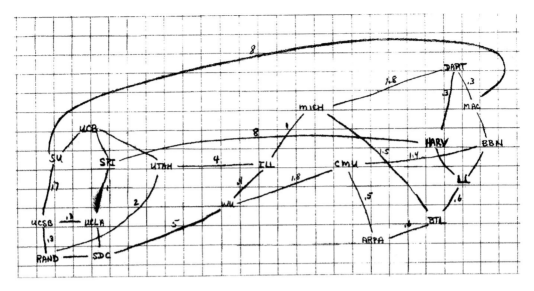

The key to this new technology was a concept called packet switching. Electronic information was broken into small pieces, or packets, that could be sent through any available network connection and reassembled once it reached its destination. If the data flow was disrupted in one part of the network, the information simply took another route. Packet switching proved to be a much faster and more reliable form of data transmission than anything that had been tried before.

The ARPANET started out with four nodes, or network intersections, that could process, store, or forward information to each other. Although network access was initially limited to research institutions and defense contractors, the ARPANET quickly outgrew its original function. Talented computer programmers came up with all sorts of new applications to make the technology serve their needs.

This diagram shows the ancestor of the modern Internet, a computer network called the ARPANET.

E-mail and Electronic Communication

In 1971 engineer Ray Tomlinson invented the first electronic mail (e-mail) program. It allowed ARPANET users to send messages to each other using a standardized online address. Each e-mail address consisted of the recipient's name and network location (or host computer), separated by the typographical symbol @. People immediately recognized that e-mail offered a quick and easy method of exchanging information, collaborating on projects, or just keeping in touch with friends. E-mail proved so popular that it accounted for 75 percent of traffic on the network within a year of its invention.

As the potential value of electronic communication became clear, researchers around the world began building their own computer networks. In 1974 two American computer scientists, Vinton Cerf and Robert Kahn, came up with a way to connect these separate, incompatible computer networks to the ARPANET. They developed what they called an "internetworking" protocol, which was a set of rules that allowed different types of networks to communicate with each other. In 1978 they discovered that the protocol worked better when it was split into two parts, transmission control protocol (TCP) and Internet protocol (IP).

TCP/IP helped the ARPANET expand even more rapidly. In 1983 it was connected to NSFNet, a computer

During the 1970s Bob Kahn and Vinton Cerf, pictured here, developed the TCP/IP, which helped the ARPANET expand even more rapidly.

Becoming a Computer Software Engineer

Job Description: Computer software engineers are responsible for designing, developing, testing, and evaluating the software programs used in computers. They are involved in the creation and maintenance of many different types of software, such as operating systems; network distribution, word processing, inventory, payroll programs, and games.

Education: A bachelor's degree in computer science, software engineering, or information systems is preferred, but not required.

Qualifications: Computer software engineers need strong analytical and problem-solving skills. Experience with a variety of computer systems and technologies, as well as knowledge of programming languages like C, C++, Java, Fortran, and COBOL, is also highly desirable.

Additional Information: To keep up with advances in technology, computer software engineers must frequently update their skills through continuing education and professional development seminars. The Association for Computing Machinery is a professional association for those in all areas of computer science and it offers career information on its Web site, www.acm.org.

Salary: $79,780 per year

network operated by the National Science Foundation that included various universities working on scientific research projects. The link between the ARPANET and NSFNet connected more than three thousand host computers into a single network. Before the end of the decade, the number of host computers on the network had exceeded one hundred thousand, and exciting new applications for this technology were being developed every day. By this time it was clear that the ARPANET had surpassed its original goal. The computer network not only extended across North America, but also reached as far as Europe and Australia. In 1992 the U.S. government ended its involvement in the project and made the network— now known as the Internet—available to the public for commercial use.

Early Online Communities

Although the ARPANET technology was not sophisticated enough to support modern social networking sites like Facebook and MySpace, early users of the network came up with many innovative ways to share information and communicate with each other. One of the first online communities was Usenet, a system created in 1979 by Duke University graduate students Tom Truscott and Jim Ellis. Usenet was a discussion forum in which members could post messages and read messages posted by other members. The online discussions were divided into categories, or newsgroups, based on members' areas of interest.

A similar method of online interaction, called a bulletin board system (BBS), was introduced in 1984. Like Usenet groups, BBS allowed members to exchange messages and information. BBS users also could download software, play games, and read postings on public message boards. Most BBS systems were hosted, meaning that all the information was stored on a central server or host computer. To access a BBS, members had to log in to the system over a telephone line using a modem. Since long-distance phone charges generally applied to these dial-up connections, BBS often catered to people within a local community. In many cases, groups that shared similar interests online arranged to meet in person. Online BBS groups thus evolved into off-line social networks.

Another important early online community was the WELL (short for Whole Earth 'Lectronic Link), created in 1985. Unlike most other discussion groups from this period, which centered around computers and technical issues, the WELL focused on current events and social issues. It attracted artists, writers, philosophers, scientists, and other intellectuals who enjoyed exchanging views and expressing opinions on various topics of interest. The wide-ranging discussions that took place on the WELL influenced the development of many later social networking sites. "[The Well] is widely known as the primordial ooze where the online community movement was born—where [technology writer and social critic] Howard Rheingold first coined the term 'virtual community,'"[3] notes the WELL's Web site.

As the WELL and other general-interest sites helped the Internet move beyond the realm of computer experts and research scientists, businesses emerged to help ordinary people connect to the growing network. In the days before the invention of the World Wide Web and browser software, navigating the Internet and locating information required users to type in complicated series of commands. As a result, novice users tended to find the technology confusing or intimidating. In the late 1980s and early 1990s, commercial online services like CompuServe, America Online (AOL), EarthLink, and Netcom stepped in to address this problem. These companies not only offered their customers easy Internet access and navigation tools, but also gave them an online destination and created a sense of community.

CompuServe, for instance, enabled its customers to read news reports, make travel reservations, and go shopping online. AOL allowed its members to interact with one another by exchanging e-mails or by joining discussion groups on a wide variety of topics. It even introduced an early version of online social networking by letting members create searchable personal profiles. These early commercial online services helped introduce millions of people to the Internet.

The World Wide Web

The innovation that made the Internet useful and accessible to ordinary people, however, was the World Wide Web. The Web is basically a program that runs on the Internet and helps users locate and retrieve information stored on the vast network. Before the Web came along, the Internet was often compared to a library in which all the books were in a huge pile, making it very difficult for anyone to find what they were looking for. The Web created a space on the Internet for sharing information that was available to network users

> **BITS & BYTES**
> **1.6 billion**
> Number of people around the world who were connected to the Internet as of March 2009 (24 percent of the global population of 6.7 billion)

worldwide. "The basic idea of the Web is that of an information space through which people can communicate . . . by sharing their knowledge in a pool,"[4] explains British scientist Tim Berners-Lee, creator of the World Wide Web.

When he invented the Web in 1991, Berners-Lee worked at CERN, an international particle physics laboratory in Switzerland. He initially wrote the program to help him remember the connections between the hundreds of scientists and research projects being carried out at that facility. Berners-Lee created a system of embedded codes called hypertext markup language (HTML) that established links between documents stored on the CERN computer system. The hypertext links appeared as highlighted text on a computer screen. When users clicked on a link, they were instantly transported to a separate document containing related information.

An example of hypertext markup language, or HTML, a system of embedded codes used to create pages on the World Wide Web.

Before long, Berners-Lee decided that his creation could help people find information on the broader Internet. On August 6, 1991, he announced his invention of the World Wide Web in a Usenet discussion group. The first Web page in history featured his explanation of HTML and the World Wide Web, along with a few sample links. Programmers around the world immediately adopted HTML and

```
<!doctype html public "-//W3C//DTD WWW HTML 3.2 Final//EN">
<html>
<head>
<title>Crash Landing in Roswell</title>
<meta name="keywords" content="Roswell, New Mexico, aliens, Air Force">
</head>
<body>
<h1>Space Invaders; Or, Weather Balloon Gone Astray?<h1>
<p>In the summer of 1947, in the desert of central New Mexico, a local rancher found some
unusual debris on his property. After authorities began to investigate the nature of the strange,
metallic material, the U.S. Air Force quickly ruled that the debris was a remnant of a downed
weather balloon. Then and today, many believe the government was trying to hide the
truth<em>that the debris was actually part of a extraterrestrial spacecraft that had crash
landed in the desert, with aliens onboard.<p>
<img src="roswell.jpg" alt="Roswell in 1947" height="350" width="500">
<p><a href="home.html">Home</a></p>
</body>
</html>
```

Inside a Wireless Router

A router is a device that directs the flow of information through a computer network. Wireless routers enable computers or mobile devices to access the Internet remotely, without the need to connect physically through cables or wires.

A wireless router, or gateway, operates using radio waves, which are a form of electromagnetic energy that can be used to carry signals. Technically, wireless routers are two-way radio communication systems, similar to cellular phones or walkie-talkies. Wireless routers use higher frequencies than these other technologies, which allows them to carry more data, and they can change frequencies rapidly in order to reduce interference.

Computers and handheld devices use wireless adapters to translate data into radio waves and transmit it through the air. Wireless routers contain ports to receive radio waves from remote computers. They decode the radio signals and transmit the data to the Internet through a wired connection. Routers also can receive data from the Internet, change it into a radio signal, and transmit it to remote computers.

In the first decade of the twenty-first century, wireless routers were used to provide Internet access in airports, hotels, shopping malls, restaurants, and libraries across the United States. In addition, many Americans set up their own wireless networks in their homes.

WIRELESS CONNECTION

Computers use wireless adaptors to translate data into radio wave signals. The wireless router receives these signals and decodes them, sending information to the Internet through a wired connection.

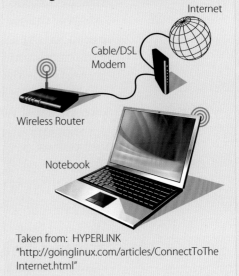

Taken from: HYPERLINK "http://goinglinux.com/articles/ConnectToThe Internet.html"

began formatting text-based documents as Web pages. Although many of these early Web sites were simple by twenty-first-century standards, they quickly multiplied and grew more sophisticated.

The next challenge for Internet users was to keep track of the growing number of interesting sites available on the World Wide Web. At first, many users kept manual lists of their favorite pages. Then some innovative users began building software programs that became known as Web browsers. Marc Andreessen created the first modern browser, called Mosaic, in 1993. Mosaic and other browser programs enabled users to store or bookmark Web pages, so they could return to favorite sites without having to type in complicated commands. Mosaic also allowed users to access the Web through a familiar, graphical interface that resembled the point-and-click icons used in the popular Microsoft Windows operating system.

The creation of Web browsers made the Internet accessible to the general public. With such a wealth of information available online, the number of computer users worldwide expanded rapidly. A number of new online communities formed around this time that catered to general interests, such as Geocities (launched in 1994) and Tripod (launched in 1995). Some of these sites allowed people to create their own, personal Web sites, known as home pages, and to interact with one another in chat rooms.

Entering the Twenty-First Century

The Internet, early online communities, the World Wide Web, and browser software all helped pave the way for the creation of modern online social networks. The final necessary ingredient was a high-speed Internet connection, which developed around the turn of the twenty-first century. In 1995 most people accessed the Internet through dial-up telephone connections and modems that transferred data at an average rate of 14.4 kilobytes per second. This slow connection speed placed severe limits on the creativity of Web page designers. Sites that featured fancy graphics took so long to load that potential visitors often ran out of patience.

But improvements in Internet technology led to a tremendous increase in average connection speeds over the next decade. By 2005 broadband links were widely available, including cable modems, digital subscriber lines (DSL), and

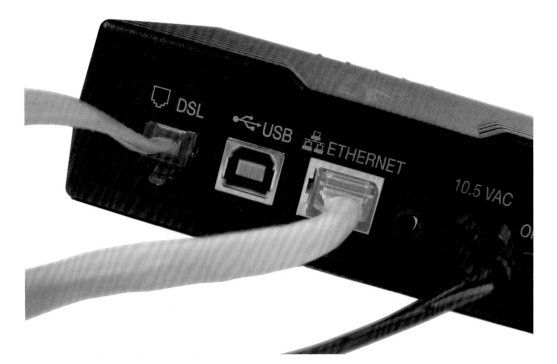

wireless fidelity (Wi-Fi). These high-speed Internet connections transferred data at an average rate of 8 megabytes per second, or five hundred times faster than the old dial-up connections. As a result, Web page designers became free to create interactive sites that featured sound, images, animation, and other enhancements.

These lively Web sites generated increased interest among users and boosted the Internet's usefulness as an educational tool, marketing device, and entertainment destination. In addition, broadband technology created opportunities for more immediate and appealing forms of social interaction than had ever been possible on the Internet before. The stage was thus set for the emergence of a new and exciting generation of online social networking sites.

Advanced technology like DSL broadband modems, allowed Web developers to create more interactive sites that featured sounds, images, and animation.

CHAPTER 2

The Development of Online Social Networks

Beginning around 1995, online social networking entered an exciting period of development and growth. Improvements in Internet technology and increases in connection speeds enabled innovative Web site designers to create a whole new generation of online communities. Instead of being organized around topics for discussion or areas of interest, these new social networking environments were organized around people. They allowed each member to become the center of his or her own community, with the ability to create a personal profile, establish connections with friends, and share information. Of course, full-service social networking sites, like Facebook and MySpace, did not appear overnight. Instead, they grew out of trial-and-error experiments by a number of Internet entrepreneurs. Many of the early social networking sites failed, but some of them contributed important new ideas that became standard elements of the sites that came later.

Social Networking Goes Online

Some of the early efforts to facilitate social networking online targeted specific groups of people. Classmates.com, for example, was intended to help people get in touch with long-lost school friends. When it was first introduced in

1995, the Web site did not allow users to create a personal profile or a home page. Instead, users registered their school affiliations and e-mail addresses in a central database. Then they could search the database for former classmates who also might be registered. The idea of reestablishing school friendships appealed to many people, and Classmates.com became an immediate hit. A decade after its introduction, it boasted 40 million active members.

A number of other early social networking sites were dedicated to helping single people find romantic partners. One of the most successful online dating services, Match .com, was founded in 1996. In exchange for a monthly fee, it allowed members to build personal profiles, search for other members who met their dating requirements, and send messages to other members. When Match.com was first introduced, many people had a negative perception of online dating. Once the idea caught on, however, business on the site took off. By 2002 Match.com controlled 25 percent of the online dating industry and took in $76 million in annual revenue.

Although targeted at a specific audience, Classmates.com became an instant hit with the online community and by 2005 boasted 40 million members.

One of the most influential early social networking sites, SixDegrees.com, was intended to help people establish relationships with friends of friends. Introduced in 1997, it was based on an idea called "six degrees of separation." This theory claimed that any two people in the world were connected to one another by a chain of friends and acquaintances consisting of fewer than six links. SixDegrees.com was one of the first Web sites that allowed members to create lists of friends and view the lists created by their friends.

SixDegrees.com included many of the basic features of modern social networking services. It allowed users to build a profile, create a list of friends, send messages to friends, view other members' profiles, search for members with shared interests, and organize their own groups. Although most of these features already existed in some form, SixDegrees.com brought them all together in one place. Nevertheless, the site failed to earn money and shut down within a few years of its introduction. Some analysts assert that SixDegrees.com simply appeared before the world was ready for it, since few Internet users had wide networks of friends and family members online at that time.

Friendster Launches the Networking Craze

The site that is widely credited with bringing online social networking into the mainstream of computer users is Friendster. Software engineer Jonathan Abrams founded the site in his San Francisco apartment in 2002. Abrams wanted to harness the power of the Internet to help people communicate and connect with each other. "The way people interacted online was either anonymous or through aliases or handles," he explains. "I wanted to bring that real-life context that you had offline online—so instead of Cyberdude 307, I would be Jonathan."[5]

Abrams took the basic elements of early social networking sites—member profiles and lists of friends—and expanded upon them. One of his major innovations was a concept

CIRCLE OF FRIENDS

Software engineer Jonathan Abrams is credited with creating a concept called "circle of friends," which presents social networking site membership networks in graphic form.

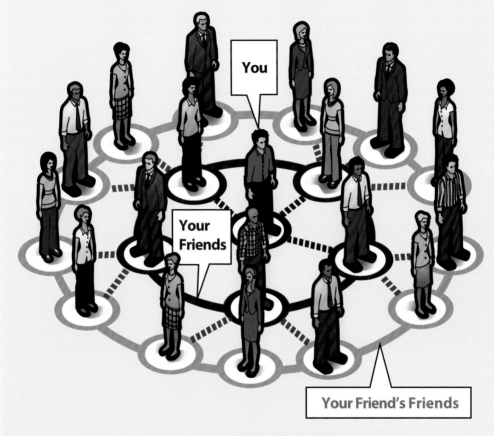

You

Your Friends

Your Friend's Friends

Taken from: HYPERLINK "http://communication.howstuffworks.com/how-online-social-networks-work6.htm"

called the "circle of friends," which showed the network of connections between members in graphical form. He also invented a way to use these social graphs to assess the compatibility between members and suggest people who might make good friends.

Abrams officially launched Friendster in March 2003. Within six months it had attracted more than 2 million members. The site received a great deal of media coverage and was often described as the hottest Internet start-up in America. To facilitate Friendster's growth, Abrams collected funding from venture capital firms and hired proven technology executives to help run the company.

Before long, though, Friendster began experiencing management conflicts. In addition, high traffic on the site caused technical problems, which left many members feeling frustrated. "Friendster should have been the preeminent social networking site out there," Internet analyst Gray Miller notes. "Unfortunately, early on it was plagued with many technical difficulties that made it difficult, if not impossible, for the users to actually interact. As a result, as much as they may have liked Friendster, they found other services where they could communicate with each other more easily."[6]

Some of Friendster's policies also angered its early members. A few imaginative users created fake profiles, known as Fakesters, that supposedly represented celebrities or fictional characters. Many people found it entertaining to view the fake profiles and interact with their creators.

Software engineer and Friendster.com founder Jonathan Abrams holds up a promotional shirt at his office in California. Friendster.com is credited with bringing online social networking to mainstream computer users.

Despite the popularity of the Fakesters, however, Friendster management decided that falsifying profiles was an unacceptable use of the site. They worried that they might be held liable if users impersonated real people, and they did not want the site to become a big joke. The company deleted all suspicious profiles and banned any users who misrepresented themselves. This policy turned many users against Friendster management.

Although Friendster's popularity faded in the United States, it remained among the top-ranked social networking sites in other parts of the world, particularly in the Philippines, Singapore, Malaysia, and Indonesia. It also had a strong influence on the development of future sites. "It was an unfortunate example of being too early in a developing market," Brian McConnell states in *GigaOM*. "Everything I have seen since Friendster is highly influenced by it, and generally offers the same basic features, just in a different package."[7] In fact, Abrams and his company received four U.S. patents for inventing fundamental technologies involved in online social networking.

MySpace Appeals to Teens

The initial success of Friendster inspired many Internet entrepreneurs to launch their own social networking sites over the next few years. Some of these sites targeted specific groups of people. Dogster gave dog owners a place to compare notes about their pets, while Care2 helped activists connect with worthy causes. LinkedIn, a networking site aimed at business professionals, launched in 2003. A resource for finding jobs, making contacts, and expanding professional relationships, the site attracted 30 million members by 2009.

The next social networking site to emerge as a major rival to Friendster was MySpace. Founded in 2003 by Tom Anderson and Chris DeWolfe, MySpace appealed directly to

Chris De Wolfe (left) and Tom Anderson (right) created a trendy online social networking site that appealed to young Internet users when they founded MySpace.

people who had become disenchanted with Friendster. For instance, the new site welcomed independent rock bands that had been kicked off of Friendster for breaking rules about profile content. Thousands of up-and-coming bands created MySpace profiles and used them as a way to promote themselves. This focus on music and entertainment gave MySpace a growing reputation as a trendy place for hip, young Internet users to hang out. "MySpace visitors listened to music, scoped out crushes, made plans with friends, decided that [Comedy Central television personality] Stephen Colbert was cool—and in the process altered the way we think about and use the Internet,"[8] Max Chafkin writes in *Inc.*

In 2004 MySpace allowed minors to become members. Teenagers rushed to join the site, and by the fall of that year MySpace boasted 22 million users. According to the authors of the book *MySpace Unraveled*:

MySpace was the turning point for social networking. It allowed users to combine the media-rich self-expression that blogging was beginning to offer with multiple socializing tools (IM, email, comments, buddy lists, discussion boards, and chat). Suddenly, there was something seemingly made to order for teens. . . . It was MySpace's embrace of both publishing and socializing tools—when it mattered when teens were looking for something even more social than blogs—that made it a traffic-growth record-breaker.[9]

MySpace's breathtaking rise to the rank of most-popular social networking site generated a great deal of media attention. The buzz surrounding the company increased further in 2005, when the site was sold for $580 million to media mogul Rupert Murdoch's News Corporation, which owns the Fox TV networks as well as newspapers, magazines, and other media. This sale marked the first time that a mainstream media company made a social networking site the focus of its Internet business strategy.

A short time later, however, MySpace began experiencing a backlash. Some members worried that the new corporate owners would change the MySpace environment, perhaps by making it more commercial. Other members grew concerned about safety issues, as news reports surfaced about sexual predators using the site to contact minors. "This is how social networks collapse," explains technology writer Vanessa Grigoriadis in *New York* magazine. "For no rational reason, a queasiness sets in, the comfort level drops, and people start to drift away. One day the numbers are growing exponentially, and the next they're stagnant, none of the users are actually showing up, and there's another network that's getting all the buzz."[10]

Facebook Rockets to the Top

In the meantime, MySpace faced ever-increasing competition from a new wave of online social networking services. A variety of new sites launched, each one hoping to become the next big hit. By 2006 Internet users had more than two hundred different social networks to choose from. In addition, social networking accounted for a progressively larger percentage of the total time people spent online. The share of U.S. Internet visits attracted by the top twenty social networking sites doubled between September 2005 and September 2006, from one out of every forty visits to one out of every twenty.

One of the sites that was introduced during this period, Facebook, would eventually replace MySpace as the world's leading online social network. Facebook originated in 2004 on the campus of Harvard University. Student Mark Zuckerberg created the site to serve as an online yearbook for his classmates. Grigoriadis describes the campus version of

Facebook differentiated itself from other online networking sites by allowing users to personalize their profiles. As a result, Facebook replaced MySpace as the number one online social networking site.

Facebook as "a space similar to a college quad, where members can check each other out, talk about culture, gossip, and pass . . . notes."[11] The site soon expanded beyond Harvard to other universities, then opened up to high school students, and finally became available to users outside of educational institutions in 2006.

Facebook differentiated itself from many other social networking sites by encouraging its members to use add-on applications created by outside developers. More than fifty thousand of these applications, also known as tools or widgets, eventually became available to enhance and personalize the Facebook experience. Members took advantage of the programs to customize their personal profiles, create charts of their travel histories, compare movie preferences with friends, and perform countless other tasks on the site.

Facebook's accessible features, ease of use, and aggressive marketing strategy helped it achieve remarkable growth. By the fall of 2007 the site boasted 50 million active users, and more than 1 million new members signed up every week. Despite its origins on a college campus, Facebook managed

Facebook Founder Mark Zuckerberg

Mark Zuckerberg, who founded Facebook as a sophomore at Harvard University in 2004, was born on May 14, 1984, in Dobbs Ferry, New York. He is the second of four children born to Edward Zuckerberg, a dentist, and Karen Zuckerberg, a psychiatrist. Zuckerberg developed an interest in computers at an early age. During his high school years at Phillips Exeter Academy in New Hampshire, he wrote a software program that evaluated people's musical tastes and developed playlists to match them.

Zuckerberg initially built the site that became Facebook to serve as an online yearbook for Harvard students. When university administrators refused to release student records for his database, he simply invited fellow students to create their own online profiles. More than half of the student body signed up on Facebook within the first two weeks.

The site's popularity convinced Zuckerberg to expand it beyond the college community. In 2005 he dropped out of school and moved to California. He found investors and built Facebook into the world's top social networking site. Zuckerberg has reportedly rejected offers of up to $1 billion for his phenomenally successful business. As chief executive officer, he establishes the strategic direction of the company and oversees technological development on the website.

Mark Zuckerberg originally built the site that has become Facebook to serve as an online yearbook for Harvard students, but its popularity convinced him to expand it beyond the college community.

to avoid being labeled as a site aimed exclusively at young people. Instead, it attracted an influx of adults over the age of thirty—most of whom were first-time users of online social networking services.

Facebook's broad appeal helped the site surpass MySpace in 2009 with 200 million members worldwide. MySpace, meanwhile, suffered a steep decline in advertising revenues and was forced to cut costs by reducing its U.S. workforce by one-third and its overseas workforce by two-thirds. "Things are moving and changing incredibly fast on the web right now," writes Grigoriadis in 2009. "Facebook's massive cultural footprint could be washed away tomorrow by forces not yet understood. . . . We keep perpetuating the cycle of birthing and abandoning new online communities, drawing close and then pulling away, on a perpetual search for the perfect balance of unity and autonomy on the web."[12]

Twitter Changes the Game

The next social networking service to make a splash on the Internet was Twitter. In 2006 creator Jack Dorsey decided to build a Web site that would enable him to get periodic updates on the status of his friends. He and his business partners, Evan Williams and Biz Stone, designed Twitter to ask the question, "What are you doing?" Users supplied quick, frequent answers to this question by sending "tweets," or short messages consisting of 140 characters or less. Twitter allowed each user to "follow" the tweets of a select list of people—including real-life friends and colleagues, celebrities, and media outlets. These people's postings automatically appeared in reverse chronological order on all of their followers' Twitter pages.

Although Twitter lacked some of the features that had become common on other social networking sites, its simplicity appealed to many people. In addition, the site's founders welcomed the input of users and third-party software developers to make the site more relevant and useful. For instance, innovative users came up with the concept of preceding tweets with names or phrases called hashtags to facilitate searching. They introduced the # symbol followed by a hashtag to designate tweets related to a specific topic or event, and the @ symbol followed by a hashtag to address tweets to specific users. Other popular outside applications allowed users to search a live stream of tweets in order to follow discussions in real time, upload photos and link to them, or create maps showing the geographic locations of other Twitter users.

The 140-character limit made Twitter easy to use on mobile phones and other handheld devices. Users could send tweets via text messaging, instant messaging, or over the Internet. Some critics complained that Twitter took the idea of social networking too far by encouraging people to share the mundane details of their daily lives. But the site's founders argued that users could choose how closely to follow updates. They also pointed out that followers did not have any obligation to respond to tweets from their friends, which made it easier for users to tune in and out of the stream of updates.

Many Twitter users added interest to their tweets by including links to online news articles, blog posts, photos,

Because Twitter is easy to use on mobile phones and other handheld devices the number of users grew rapidly in just a year's time. The site was not only popular with ordinary people, but with celebrities and the media as well.

or videos. Twitter's real-time search function also enabled large groups of people to carry on live online chats about virtually any topic, from the U.S. presidential debates to the season finales of popular television shows. Finally, Twitter proved to be useful for spreading the word quickly about up-to-the-minute events, from impromptu appearances by rock bands to political protests.

The number of Twitter users grew rapidly, from 1.7 million in May 2008 to 19.7 million a year later. This rapid growth generated a huge amount of media attention, and Twitter was often cited as the future direction of social networking. Although some critics predicted that Twitter would be a passing fad, others argued that it had fundamentally changed the nature of online social networking. "The key elements of the Twitter platform—the follower structure, link sharing,

Web 2.0

The rise of online social networking coincided with the development of a concept known as Web 2.0. Web 2.0 is not a new or updated version of the World Wide Web. Instead, the term is used to describe an evolution in Web content and interactivity that created what one Internet guide describes as "the everywhere, all-the-time, multimedia, multidevice, downloadable and uploadable, user-driven Internet."

One significant development in Web 2.0 is that designers increasingly use the Web as a platform for software applications. For many years, the Web served mainly as an information storage facility. Web 2.0, in contrast, serves a broader purpose. Web designers build a wide variety of applications that are accessible through Web browsers, including word processors, spreadsheets, photo editors, and games.

Another way that online content has evolved in Web 2.0 is that it has become more interactive, user-driven, and participatory. Instead of simply reading the news online, for example, Web 2.0 allows people to post comments on news sites, engage in dialogue about issues on blogs, and raise awareness by sharing information with friends on social networking sites.

Larry Magid and Anne Collier, *MySpace Unraveled: A Parent's Guide to Teen Social Networking*, Berkeley, CA: Peachpit Press, 2007, p. 1.

real-time searching—will persevere regardless of Twitter's fortunes," analyst Gray Miller writes. "In fact, every major channel of information will be Twitterfied in one way or another in the coming years."[13]

Social Media Sites Let People Share

As the popularity of social networking services continued to grow, it became clear that people wanted their online connections with friends to involve more than just communicating with words. They wanted to share photographs, videos, music, news stories, book and movie reviews, and favorite Web sites as well. Many social networking sites added features designed to help members share content. Others established cooperative relationships with media-sharing sites that already offered these services.

YouTube, for example, enabled people to upload, share, and watch original video clips. Founded in 2005, the site became such an immediate success that it was acquired by Google within a year of its introduction. By 2009 YouTube was the third most-visited site on the Internet, with more daily visitors than Facebook. Another popular site launched in 2005, Flickr, helped people manage and share collections of personal photographs. Blog-hosting sites like Xanga, LiveJournal, and Blogger made it easy for ordinary people—without any experience in computer programming or Web-site design—to create their own online diaries or journals.

As the amount of user-generated content expanded, the lines separating online media sharing from social networking blurred even further. Many sites that focused on media sharing added some of the same features found on online social networks. YouTube and Flickr, for example, allowed users to create communities or groups of subscribers for sharing photos or videos. Alternatively, members of Facebook could use their profiles to show videos found on YouTube. As the competition for users' time and attention heated up, all of these sites tried to anticipate users' changing tastes and preferences and provide a dynamic environment for social interaction.

CHAPTER 3

How Online Social Networks Work

B y 2009 the most popular online social networking services boasted millions of members around the world, offered a variety of interesting features, and received a great deal of media attention. In the most basic terms, however, they were simply Web sites on the Internet. The technology behind Facebook, MySpace, and Twitter was quite similar to that driving the nearly 200 million other Web sites available online. Understanding how the larger Internet works can provide a new perspective on the interactions involved in online social networking.

Communication on the Internet

The Internet is a giant network of computer networks that makes it possible for any computer in the world to communicate with any other computer. Home computers access the Internet by using a dial-up telephone connection, a dedicated service line (DSL), a cable modem, or a wireless fidelity (Wi-Fi) system and an Internet service provider (ISP). Schools and offices, on the other hand, usually link all of their computers together into a local-access network (LAN), which then accesses an ISP host through a high-speed connection.

Local ISPs maintain a central computer called a point of presence (POP) server that gives users in the surrounding area access to company's network. These local servers are connected, in turn, to regional servers operated by larger ISPs. The very largest ISPs are major communications businesses that maintain huge, high-speed networks known as the backbones of the Internet. These backbones, which can serve entire countries or parts of the world, are connected to each other through fiber-optic cables or satellite links. Although no one owns the Internet, and there is no central authority that requires ISPs to participate, the companies agree to connect their backbones for the benefit of users everywhere. The points where the different backbones meet are called network access points (NAPs), and they control the flow of trillions of bytes of data.

Information that flows through the Internet can reach its destination in a fraction of a second thanks to special computers called routers. Routers are capable of analyzing the thousands of possible paths between one computer and another and choosing the most efficient way to send messages. They also prevent messages from going through other networks unnecessarily, which helps speed up the flow of data.

BITS & BYTES
85,500 years

Total amount of time spent by users worldwide on social networking sites and blogs in December 2008

Domain Names and URLs

The different computer networks that make up the Internet communicate with each other using a standard set of rules called Internet protocol (IP). Every computer that is connected to the Internet has its own, unique IP address, which consists of a long string of numbers. The central servers that process information usually have a fixed IP address. Individual users on home computers, known as clients, are generally assigned a temporary IP address for the duration of their Internet visit. Information stored on various computers around the world can be accessed through their IP addresses.

The Domain Name System, or DNS, was developed by computer experts as an easy way for people to remember locations on the Internet.

Since numeric IP addresses are difficult for people to remember, computer experts came up with the Domain Name System (DNS) in 1983. The DNS allowed computer users to refer to locations on the Internet using words rather than numbers. Special computers called DNS servers simply translated the domain names back to machine-readable IP addresses.

Internet domain names, also known as uniform resource locators (URLs), consist of several pieces of information. The first part, "http," denotes hypertext transfer protocol, the set of rules used to transmit messages over the Internet. The second part, usually "www" for World Wide Web, describes the location of the host computer. The next part is the name of the server where the information resides—for example, "umich" for the University of Michigan—followed by a period or "dot" and a three-letter, top-level domain code. These domains divide Internet sites into different categories, such as ".com" for commercial sites, ".org" for nonprofit or charitable organizations, ".edu" for educational institutions, and ".gov" for government entities.

Pages on the World Wide Web

Each URL refers to a specific location on the Internet that contains information. The World Wide Web is the space on the Internet where most of this information resides. The information is generally stored as Web pages, or specially formatted files or documents that contain text, graphics, and other elements.

Web pages are created using a computer programming code called hypertext markup language (HTML). In order to display a Web page, a computer uses a software program known as a Web browser to translate the HTML codes into instructions about how to format the information on the screen. Some of the most commonly used browser programs are Microsoft Internet Explorer, Netscape Navigator, and Mozilla Firefox.

When a computer user types a URL into a Web browser, the browser software sends the information to a DNS server, which translates it into an IP address. This address is used to locate and contact the server where the appropriate Web page is stored. The Web browser requests the file containing

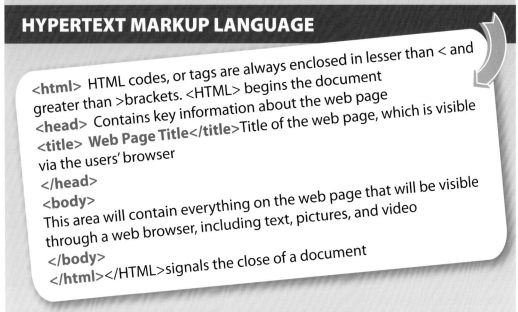

HYPERTEXT MARKUP LANGUAGE

<html> HTML codes, or tags are always enclosed in lesser than < and greater than >brackets. <HTML> begins the document

<head> Contains key information about the web page

<title> Web Page Title</title>Title of the web page, which is visible via the users' browser

</head>

<body>
This area will contain everything on the web page that will be visible through a web browser, including text, pictures, and video

</body>

</html></HTML>signals the close of a document

Taken from: HYPERLINK "http://www.web-source.net/html_codes_chart.htm"

Becoming a Web Designer

Job Description: Web designers create the pages that form a Web site. They often participate in the planning, layout, and organization of a site, including the choice of typeface, color scheme, and images. In addition to making the pages look appealing on a computer screen, designers must arrange the pages for accessibility, ease of use, and functionality. Web designers can work for a large company or as an independent contractor for a variety of clients.

Education: A bachelor's degree in computer science, graphic design, business administration, or marketing is preferred, but not required.

Qualifications: Designers are often required to possess knowledge or training in certain programming languages—especially hypertext markup language (HTML) and JavaScript—as well as training in such computer graphics packages as Dreamweaver and Photoshop.

Additional Information: The HTML Writers Guild offers training and certification for web designers at http://www.hwg.org.

Salary: $59,894 per year

the Web page, and the server responds by sending the HTML codes for the page back to the browser. The browser then decodes the HTML and uses it to format the document on the user's computer screen.

Web Sites Become More Interactive

A Web site is a collection of related Web pages that are linked together. All of the files that make up a Web site are usually stored together on a host server—a large, central computer operated by the owner of the Web site or by an ISP. Web sites are usually structured so that the URL takes users to the home page, which describes the information available on the rest of the site. In this way, the home page acts like a table of contents in a book, and the remaining pages contain the details. The pages of a Web site are connected through hyperlinks, or embedded HTML codes that provide instructions to open a new Web page. Hyperlinks usually appear as underlined text on a computer screen.

```
function panels_menu() {
  $items = array();
  // Provide some common options to reduce code repetition.
  $base = array(
    'access arguments' => array('access content'),
    'type' => MENU_CALLBACK,
    'file' => 'includes/display-edit.inc',
  );

  $items['panels/ajax/add-pane'] = array(
    'page callback' => 'panels_ajax_add_pane_choose'
  ) + $base;
  $items['panels/ajax/add-pane-config'] = array(
    'page callback' => 'panels_ajax_add_pane_conf
  + $base;
  tems['panels/ajax/configure'] = array(
  page callback' => 'panels_ajax_configure_pa
  $base;
  ms['panels/ajax/show']
```

AJAX programming language, shown here, allows web designers to create sites with even more dynamic content and reduces the amount of communication necessary between the web browser and server.

Early Web sites consisted mostly of text and did not allow users to interact with the page. This situation began to change in the late 1990s, when innovative programmers developed ways to increase the power of Web browsers. Instead of simply interpreting HTML codes and displaying documents, these enhanced browsers could perform a wide range of new functions. The introduction of plug-in software applications like Adobe Flash Player, for instance, enabled Web browsers to play multimedia content on Web sites. Similarly, the development of programming languages like JavaScript allowed Web browsers to display interactive features, such as images that change when the cursor moves over them.

JavaScript formed the basis for the AJAX (Asynchronous JavaScript and XML) programming language. Released in 2005, it allows Web designers to create sites with even more dynamic content. The main benefit of AJAX is that it reduces the amount of communication necessary between a Web browser and server. When a browser requested a Web page under the old model, the server returned the full HTML code for that page. Every time the user interacted with the page in some way—perhaps by clicking on a graphic element or by filling in blanks on a form—the browser sent the entire page back to the server, which processed the changes and returned a rebuilt page to the browser. This exchange consumed a lot of time and processing capacity.

With AJAX, however, the server only sends the full page the first time the browser requests it. It also downloads a set of JavaScript files called the AJAX engine. From this point on, all interactions between the user and the Web page are handled by the AJAX engine, which requests small bits of information from the server as they are needed by the user. The engine then displays the changes without reloading the whole page. By limiting the amount of information that passes back and forth between client and server, AJAX provides a much more responsive interface. From the user's perspective, it appears that the changes are displayed immediately. AJAX and other technological developments helped Web designers create the dynamic content found in popular social networking sites.

Social Networking Sites

Social networking sites like Facebook and MySpace operate on the same basic principles as other Web sites, but on a much larger scale. As of 2008, for example, Facebook operated ten thousand high-capacity servers to store and process information for its millions of users around the world.

User profiles are the Web pages that make up social networking Web sites. Whenever a new member joins a social networking service, the first thing he or she must do is create a profile. Most sites provide a simple form for users to fill out online. They are asked to answer a series of questions about their age, relationship status, hometown, schools attended, hobbies, and interests. This information is sent over the Internet to the social networking site's server, where it is fed into a standard template to generate a profile, or home page, for the user.

The next step in joining a social networking service is to create a list of friends. Most sites use a sophisticated search function to pick up data in a new member's profile and compare it to data in existing members' profiles. When a new member indicates hobbies or schools attended, for instance, the search function will identify other members with the same interests or school affiliations. Many sites also offer new members the option of checking to see whether anyone in their e-mail address book has already created a profile.

Once a new user has located other members on the system to add to their friends list, most social networking sites establish links between the friends' profiles. The links make it easier for friends to share information on the site. They can upload photos and videos, view each other's albums, post comments, send instant messages, or chat online. Some sites calculate the connections between users to several degrees of separation and display the information as a social graph. When the pioneering social networking site Friendster first

Once deciding to join a social networking site, such as Facebook, a person must sign up to create a unique profile.

The Most Popular Social Networking Sites in America

According to the Internet usage tracking service Compete.com, the top-five social networking sites in the United States as of May 2009, based on number of visits, are:

1. Facebook
2. MySpace
3. Twitter
4. Flixster
5. LinkedIn

introduced this function, Max Chafkin notes in *Inc.* that "the effect was to give users a vivid sense of how they fit into their social groups as well as into the larger world."[14]

Social networking sites differ in the amount of privacy they afford their members. Some sites are accessible to anyone on the Internet, whether or not they are members. But most sites require people to sign up and create a profile before they can access information. Some sites allow members to view the profiles of all other members, while others require users to become friends before they can look at each other's profiles. Many sites give members a variety of privacy options to choose from regarding the information contained in their own profiles.

Customization and Applications

Signing up for a social networking service offers an easy way for people with no computer programming experience to create their own Web pages. Users also can change or update the information stored in their personal profiles at any time by using simple menu options. But some users find that the standard home page they can build on a social networking site does not sufficiently express their individuality. After all, other members' basic profiles look very similar. Some social networking sites have responded to this complaint by giving users the option to modify or customize their profiles in ways that better reflect their personalities.

Beyond the tools and features available from the social networking service, the main way to customize a profile is to embed HTML codes. HTML is the programming language used by Web designers to construct Web pages. Users can insert HTML codes that modify the look and feel of their profiles in various ways. They might change the background color, for instance, or add multimedia features, like music, photos, videos, and

animation. People without HTML programming skills can still customize their profiles using free online HTML code generators. After creating and testing the code on a generator Web site, they can simply copy it and paste it into their home page.

For users with more technical ability, some social networking services offer access to an application programming interface. This allows members to develop their own small software programs, known as applications or widgets, using the host site as a platform. An example of an application might be a pop-up window that invites friends to participate in an online survey. People who develop interesting applications often make them available to other members on the system. Many outside software developers also create applications for members of social networking services to use. When a Facebook user clicks on an application icon, for instance, their Web browser goes to a special space on the site called a canvas page. Application developers can use the canvas page to share information, advertise services, or sell products.

A man showing a Twitter application that allows him to personalize his Twitter page. Social networking sites allow people with no computer experience to create unique Web pages on their own.

Although adding applications can help make profiles fun and different, too much customization also can make profiles seem cluttered and difficult to navigate. In the worst cases, modifications can cause browsers to freeze up from improper coding or create security risks by linking to dangerous Web sites.

Mobile Social Networking

Many social networking sites allow members to access their profiles and interact with other members through mobile devices like cellular phones. Since mobile devices generally have less memory and processing power than computers, they are not able to interpret the HTML coding in complex Web pages. Instead, mobile devices typically use simpler programming languages that are easier to interpret, such as extensible hypertext markup language (XHTML).

Text messages sent from mobile devices to social networking sites use a standard transfer method called short message service (SMS). Such messages pass through a mobile switching center to a signal transfer point (STP), where they enter the Internet and are transmitted to the appropriate Web site. When a social networking site sends a message to a mobile device, the process is reversed. Users of social networking sites can use mobile text messaging to look up profile information, post messages, or add friends.

SMS has some limitations, however. SMS can only handle messages up to a maximum of 160 characters in length. To get around this problem, innovative programmers created the multimedia messaging service (MMS). MMS has no size limit, so it allows for the transfer of nontext messages and mobile uploads of sound, video, and image files. Receiving multimedia messages requires an MMS compatible device, however, and only advanced 3G phone networks can send very large messages.

Some social networking environments, like Twitter, are designed specifically to take advantage of mobile technology. Twitter users send short, 140-character text messages called tweets to networks of followers through SMS transfers. Twitter's developers imposed the 140-character limit in order to make the service compatible with the largest possible number of mobile devices. To allow for the mass broadcasting of tweets to a large group of followers, Twitter relies on Web syndication formats like really simple syndication (RSS). RSS is an application—consisting of a few lines of code embedded in a Web page—that is used to distribute frequently updated content, such as news feeds, blog postings, and podcasts. RSS gathers information from one source and sends it out to various destinations. Followers who subscribe to a certain Twitter user's syndication service, or feed, automatically receives an update every time that person tweets.

Like other social networking sites, Twitter encourages users to create their own applications to customize or improve upon Twitter's services. As a result, Twitter users have created thousands of applications to help people manage, organize, and follow tweets. Some examples of third-party applications that incorporate Twitter's services include feed readers that appear on a computer desktop, functions that enable searching of feeds in real time, and maps that provide a graphical representation of Twitter posts traveling around the world.

CHAPTER 4

How Online Social Networks Are Used

The various technical features on online social networking sites are designed to be very easy to use. The tools provided by popular services make it simple for anyone—even those without much computer experience—to build a profile, create a friend list, send messages, share photos and videos, and interact with other users. This ease of use helps social networking appeal to a wide audience, from teenagers and college students to musical groups, business professionals, political leaders, and social activists. Although their goals may be different, members of these groups all rely on social networking sites to connect with others and share information.

Types of Social Networks

There are many different types of online social network sites available. Closed, or gated, sites are small, internal social networks that consist of people within a particular company, association, educational institution, or other organization. Members of these networks typically use them to build relationships, organize events, and share notes from meetings. Some of the most popular social networking sites started out as closed sites and expanded their membership over time.

Open or external sites like Facebook and MySpace are the most common and best-known type of social network. Although they are open to anyone, some of these sites still target people with certain characteristics or interests. There are sites aimed at demographic groups, such as mothers of small children or people with disabilities, and sites aimed at geographic regions. A few sites started out as general in scope but were increasingly adopted by members of a certain group. Friendster, for instance, was launched in the United States but ended up attracting the majority of its membership from Asia and the Pacific Islands.

Every social network has its own look, feel, and culture, with different rules and etiquette guiding the interaction between members. Most sites allow new members to join for free. Many people maintain profiles on several sites that serve different purposes. An individual might join LinkedIn to network with professional contacts, for instance, but also establish a profile on Facebook to keep in touch with family and friends.

Security Risks on Social Networking Sites

Just like visiting any other Web site, visiting social networking sites can expose a user's computer to security threats. Computer hackers attacked several popular sites in 2009, including Facebook, MySpace, Twitter, and LinkedIn. Computer criminals also targeted users of these services with phishing schemes—official-looking messages designed to get them to reveal personal information.

Criminals also have developed new ways to use social networking sites to spread viruses or malicious software programs known as malware. They send out messages on Twitter, for instance, that encourage users to click on a link to a related site. When users follow these instructions, the link installs malware on the user's computer that allows hackers to gain access to the users' computer network. Such security threats contribute to decisions by many businesses and government agencies to prohibit their employees from using social networking sites at work.

Joining a Social Network

While online social networks vary in many ways, the process of becoming a member tends to be fairly standard and straightforward regardless of the site. The first step in joining any network is to sign up and create a profile. Most sites allow new users to begin this process by simply clicking an icon that appears on their home page. From there, prospective members are usually asked to fill out an online form that provides basic information for their profile, such as name, e-mail address, date of birth, and hometown. Next, new users are required to read the site's terms and conditions and click a button to indicate that they agree to abide by them. Once this initial sign-up process is complete, the user usually receives confirmation of membership.

New members are then given the option of personalizing their profiles with additional information. Most social networking sites provide space for members to include information about their relationship status, education, career, and

Some social online networking sites target a specific group of people, such as mothers with small children.

hobbies, as well as lists of favorite books, movies, and quotations. Most sites also request that new users upload a photograph to accompany their profiles. They offer step-by-step instructions that make it easy to transfer any digital photo file onto the site.

The next step is creating a list of friends. Most sites offer an option for new users to automatically notify everyone in their e-mail address list about their new profile and invite them to join the network as well. New members also can use a search function on the site to find friends who might already be members. In many cases, friends will see their profiles and contact them. Finally, many sites calculate the similarities between different members' profiles and lists of friends and use this information to suggest potential contacts.

A friend request is typically made by e-mail. The recipient must choose whether to accept, deny, ignore, or respond to the friend request with a message. Most social networking services require both parties to agree to be friends before their profiles can be linked.

After building a profile and creating a list of friends, new members should review their account settings and the options available to control the privacy of their information. Most social networking sites provide privacy controls that allow each user to decide who can view their profile or contact them. Some also offer ways for members to prevent their personal information from being made available to advertisers and other third parties.

Hanging Out Online

Most social networking sites give their members access to a number of common features. They allow members, for example, to send status updates to everyone on their list of friends. They also provide space for members to

TEENS WHO HAVE PROFILES ONLINE

Teens of all ages have created online profiles, but older girls are the most likely to have posted a profile online.

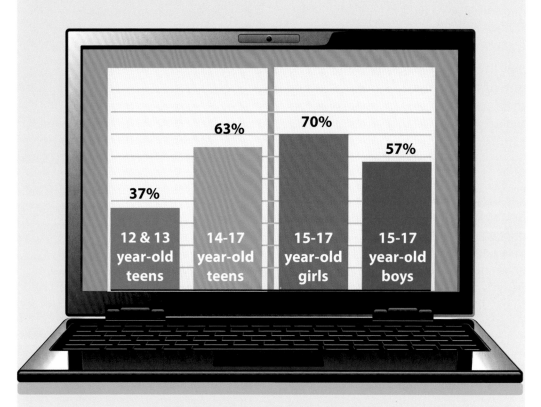

Taken from: Lenhart, Amanda and Mary Madden. Social Networking Websites and Teens. Pew Internet & American Life Project, January 7, 2007, HYPERLINK "http://www.pewinternet.org/Reports/2007/Social-Networking-Websites-and-Teens/Data-Memo/More-details-from-the-survey.aspx?r=1" http://www.pewinternet.org/Reports/2007/Social-Networking-Websites-and-Teens/Data-Memo/More-details-from-the-survey.aspx?r=1, accessed on October 30, 2009

create and share online galleries of photos. Most sites enable members to view their friends' profiles and comment on their photos or status updates. Another frequently offered feature is instant messaging (IM), which allows members to chat online with friends who are logged in at the same time.

A teen using Facebook to chat with his friends. Most young people use social networking sites to talk with their friends when they are unable to meet in person.

Different people use social networks in different ways depending on their age, relationship status, education, career, lifestyle, and other factors. For teenagers, social networks provide a familiar, interactive, collaborative space to hang out online. Many teens use social networking sites to socialize with their friends at times when they are unable to get together in person. They read and respond to comments on their own profiles, post comments on their friends' profiles, or chat online.

Other teenagers use social networking sites as a place to express themselves and experiment with different identities. Some teens spend a lot of time decorating their profiles, using changes in typeface, graphics, music, and photos to reflect their mood or personality. Teens who enjoy expressing their thoughts and feelings in writing often spend their time blogging, or updating online journals. Young poets, photographers, and artists sometimes use social networks to showcase their talents, while musicians use the sites to debut new songs and publicize performances.

Many teens join online groups or communities in which members share a particular interest, such as music, movies, games, sports, or politics. Most social networking sites also enable members to form their own groups. A sports team might use this feature to post statistics or practice schedules, while a study group could use it to share notes. High school students can use social networks to research potential colleges by connecting with students, administration, or faculty at the institution.

Surveys show that more than 90 percent of American teenagers primarily use social networking sites to socialize with off-line friends rather than to meet new people. They tend to view their favorite site as a big party at which they hang out with their usual group of friends, even though there are lots of other people in the room.

Networking for Business Professionals

While teenagers and college students were among the earliest adopters of online social networking technology, it was not long before the phenomenon spread to other segments of society. Enterprising businesspeople, for instance, recognized that online communities held a great deal of potential as tools for career advancement. By connecting people with similar career goals or business needs, social networking sites could help professionals find jobs, hire employees, collaborate on projects, or market new products.

As of 2009, LinkedIn was the leading social network aimed at business professionals. The site boasted more

BITS & BYTES

35 to 49

Age group that is the fastest-growing demographic among users of online social networks

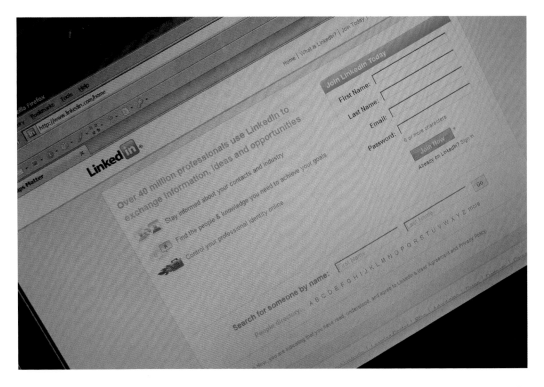

than 40 million members working in 170 industries in 200 countries around the world. Member profiles on LinkedIn tended to be straightforward and businesslike, emphasizing work experience, career goals, and professional contacts. "Whether you're a job seeker, consultant, entrepreneur, or happily employed, LinkedIn can be an incredible asset for your career," writes Dan Schawbel in *Mashable: The Social Media Guide.* "LinkedIn is not just a virtual resume that should be tucked away for a rainy day. Instead it acts as a resume, cover letter, references document, database of your contacts throughout your life and a place where you can learn, share and interact in a professional manner."[15]

In addition to sites like LinkedIn, more general social networking sites proved useful to businesspeople as well. Some companies, for example, use social networking profiles as part of their screening process for potential new employees. Recruiters can search various sites for job candidates' profiles, look at their photos, read their blog posts, and reject them if they find any objectionable content.

LinkedIn is a social networking site aimed at business professionals and allows these people to find jobs, hire employees, collaborate on projects, and market new projects.

An increasing number of businesses set up profiles on popular social networking sites as a means of connecting with their customers. Several large retailers, for instance, have established a presence on Facebook or Twitter to send out coupons or advertise special deals for their friends and followers. A number of airlines also have used the technology to offer last-minute deals on flights. They send out messages on Twitter that give followers a brief window of opportunity to take advantage of deeply discounted airfares to popular destinations. This marketing strategy reflects the industry's recognition that online social networks provide easy access to demographic groups with the income and flexible lifestyle to fill the bargain seats.

Political Campaigning

Social networking sites also have proven to be extremely useful to candidates running for political office, particularly during the 2008 elections. By this time, the Internet had expanded its reach to include nearly every segment of American society. "[During the 2004 campaign] it was limited what people were doing online—maybe they were searching, maybe they participated in forums, maybe some people belonged to Meetup and had their MySpace page," explains digital media consultant Devora Rogers. "Now, grandmothers and grandfathers are on Facebook. Teenagers and tweens are on Facebook."[16]

During the 2008 election season candidates at all levels took advantage of social networking sites to reach voters. However, presidential Democratic nominee Barack Obama was highly successful at making a comprehensive Internet strategy one of the key elements of his campaign. The architect of this strategy was Facebook cofounder Chris Hughes, who left the company in early 2007 to join the Obama campaign. Hughes ensured that the campaign made full use of emerging digital technologies and social media to connect with supporters and encourage high voter turnout.

Inspired by the example of Facebook, Obama launched his own online social network, MyBarackObama.com, for grassroots campaign organizing. Becoming a member of the

Not Making Any Money

Although social networking sites like Facebook and MySpace proved to be phenomenally successful at attracting members, few of the popular sites managed to earn profits through 2008. Instead, most sites relied upon investors to fund their operations. This situation has prompted some business analysts to question the long-term financial prospects of online social networking companies.

The main problem facing these Internet businesses is finding ways to earn money from their services. Most social networking sites do not charge members to join, maintain a profile, or connect with friends. Since people have grown accustomed to using the sites for free, they seem likely to resist any future efforts to impose fees.

Many social networking sites have attempted to earn money by charging other businesses for advertising space. Advertising on social networks appeals to some businesses because the personal data in member profiles enables them to target their ads. But other businesses have expressed concern that placing ads on social networks could harm their reputations if the ads appear alongside questionable user-generated content. Social networking sites also face pressure to limit advertising, because excessive or intrusive ads can alienate members and cause them to choose a different service.

network enabled supporters to receive updates, join local groups, organize events, and set up fund-raising pages. By the end of the campaign, volunteers had created more than 2 million profiles on the site, organized 200,000 campaign events, and raised $30 million on personal fund-raising pages. Some experts, like Patrick Patullo of *DMB: Digital Media Buzz,* claim that the site revolutionized the use of the Internet as a campaign tool. "For those who study the Internet, [the 2008 election] may be seen as a dividing line," he writes. "There will be online campaigns before 2008 and then there will be everything that comes after."[17]

The Obama campaign also maintained a Facebook page for the candidate, mobilized supporters by sending tweets on Twitter, distributed updates and fund-raising requests via e-mail, and used an iPhone application to ask volunteers to

By launching his own online social network, MyBarackObama .com, Democratic presidential candidate Barack Obama made the Internet one of the key elements of his successful campaign strategy.

call friends in battleground states. Obama's integrated social media strategy helped him raise an incredible $600 million in campaign funds, with more than $2 million individual donations coming in increments of less than $200 each. Some observers claim that it also helped make the election process more democratic by giving ordinary citizens a voice.

Social Activism

Social networking sites also played a role in promoting the interests of ordinary citizens by serving as a forum for social activism. As the reach of the Internet broadened, the technology proved to have a remarkable capacity to circulate information to a vast audience. In fact, many writers compared this function of the Internet to a virus, since information spread so quickly online. Videos, news stories, rumors, conspiracies, and even jokes were said to "go viral" when they were viewed by millions of people within a matter of hours.

Social activists took advantage of the viral nature of the Internet to raise awareness of issues and organize events, demonstrations, or boycotts of products. The technology empowered Internet-savvy young people by giving them a collective voice that resonated with political leaders. "Technology has given today's teen activists new ways to organize around issues they care about," notes Anastasia Goodstein in *Totally Wired*. "More young people get information about volunteering and social causes from the Internet than from any other media source."[18]

In recognition of this trend, many nonprofit organizations devoted to such issues as environmental protection, consumer advocacy, civil rights, and humanitarian aid set up profiles on social networking sites. These organizations use the networks to spread information about their causes to thousands of members, who in turn relay the information to a multitude of other potential supporters. In addition, online communities like YouthNoise and TakingITGlobal help connect young activists with deserving organizations to advance social causes.

BITS & BYTES

3 hours and 10 minutes

Amount of time an average user spends each month checking and updating their online social network profiles

Political Protest

By providing a forum for discussion and organization, online social networks also have emerged as an important tool in social and political protests. In 2006 for example, thousands of Hispanic students chose to walk out of class in California's largest school district despite the risk of disciplinary action. They took part in a "day without immigrants" demonstration, organized on MySpace, to protest against proposed restrictions on immigration. The protest eventually involved a hundred thousand students, about one-fourth of the district's enrollment.

Online social networks also provide a forum for political debate. In early 2009 thousands of heated exchanges erupted on these sites when Israel launched a series of military attacks against Palestinian occupants of the Gaza Strip. Some Facebook members used an application that added a running total of the deaths in Gaza to their daily status updates. This information automatically appeared on the "walls" of

Social activists have begun using the power of online social sites to raise awareness, organize events, and demonstrations, such as this Facebook rally against transit price increases and service cuts in New York in April 2009.

their entire network of friends, and thus came to the attention of millions of people around the world whenever they logged into their Facebook accounts. Many people who were sympathetic toward Israel responded with comments stating that the military offensive was justified. This situation marked a significant shift in the usual tone of discussion on Facebook. "Social-networking websites . . . started out as online cliques where friends could swap opinions on music, pop culture, and other bits of innocuous personal trivia," Deena Guzder writes in *Time.* But "sites like Facebook are increasingly being used to express political views, adding an acrimonious, even menacing undertone to what were once lighthearted online forums."[19]

Social networking sites also emerged as a source of up-to-the-minute political news and information. In June 2009 the people of Iran erupted in protest following a controversial national election in which the results were widely believed to be fixed in favor of the ruling party. Twitter users played a major role in disseminating information about the protests in

Iran to people around the world, including the international news media. Although the Iranian government attempted to censor citizens' access to the social networking site, users found ways to keep the lines of communication open. Historian Clay Shirky says, "This is the first revolution that has been catapulted onto a global stage and transformed by social media." He continues:

> People throughout the world are not only listening but responding. They're engaging with individual participants, they're passing on their messages to their friends, and they're even providing detailed instructions to enable web proxies [servers that disguise the identity and location of someone sending a message] allowing Internet access that the authorities can't immediately censor. That kind of participation is really extraordinary.[20]

Online social networks thus serve the needs of their various user groups in a variety of ways, from simple socializing and business networking to political campaigning and social activism. As the reach of the Internet continues to expand, users seem certain to develop new and exciting applications for the technology in the future.

CHAPTER 5

Impact and Implications of the Technology

Online social networking has clearly made an enormous impact on modern society. The technology has enabled diverse groups of people to form connections and share information. In addition, the appeal of online social networks attracted millions of new users to the Internet and helped it enter the mainstream of modern life. Like many other technological breakthroughs, however, online social networks are not always used wisely. Some people spend too much time on the sites at the expense of real-world relationships. Others have experienced difficulty protecting the privacy of their information online. Finally, some users have become the victims of hurtful or even criminal activity, such as cyberstalking and cyberbullying.

Overuse and Isolation

As networking sites increased the appeal of Internet use as a social pastime, reports of overuse of the technology also proliferated. Social researchers and mental-health professionals recognized a growing trend toward compulsive use of the Internet for social interaction. They acknowledge that many people spend time on social networking sites customizing their profiles, posting status updates, checking and responding to messages, visiting chat rooms, or browsing other users'

Addiction and overuse of online social networks has intensified with the widespread availability of Internet-enabled cellular phones. These phones allow people to check their profiles anywhere including restaurants, movie theaters, and business meetings.

profiles without experiencing any problems. But they also warn that some people become so reliant upon online social networking that they neglect various aspects of their off-line existence, such as their jobs, families, and health.

Although most people are able to enjoy social networking in moderation, a small percentage of users have trouble controlling the amount of time they spend online. Some psychologists compare the compulsion to visit social networking sites to addictive behaviors, like gambling. People who are addicted to social networking often come to prefer online communication to face-to-face communication. They spend an inordinate amount of time on the computer because it allows them to control social interactions, plan responses, and avoid many of the potential pitfalls involved in direct personal contact. "Are we really networking in a social sense," asks a writer for *Digital Trends,* "or are we just hiding behind our keyboards and building lists of virtual friends rather than getting out there in the real world?"[21]

The problem of addiction or overuse of online social networks has intensified with the widespread availability of Internet-enabled cellular phones and handheld electronic devices. These mobile technologies give users full-time access to social networking sites. Millions of people take advantage of this unlimited access to constantly check their profiles or send out messages. Some people visit social networks while walking down the street, sitting in a movie theater, eating in a restaurant, or attending a business meeting. A May 2009 study conducted by the Internet consulting firm Gravitytank found that application-enabled cell-phone owners spend an average of two hours per day using their devices. During some of this time, the survey found, their attention is glued to the screen at the expense of family, friends, or business associates. "When the technology's interfering with your real life, you've taken it too far," declares social networking pioneer Jonathan Abrams. "When you're having a meeting with somebody, and instead of listening to you, they're looking down at their Blackberry, is that really a benefit?"[22]

The increasing use of mobile devices at parties, restaurants, and other traditional venues for socializing has generated a great deal of criticism as well. Opponents argue that inappropriate use of social networking technology actually serves to isolate people, rather than to connect them. "What good does it do our society to take us away from a close, physical community and put us in touch with distant strangers?" asks Internet critic Clifford Stoll. "The things people yearn for most—a community, a relationship with commitment and trust—are exactly what you don't have online."[23]

But supporters claim that it is unfair to judge the value of online social networks based on the small percentage of people who overuse them. They point out that online communication creates a sense of community for many people, including some who might otherwise feel isolated. People who are extremely shy, for instance, sometimes feel more comfortable opening up and forming friendships in the virtual world. Similarly, people with physical disabilities frequently use social networks to connect with friends and relatives whom they are unable to visit in real life. Finally, teenagers who feel different or isolated from their peers can share their experiences with sympathetic listeners online

and gain a sense of belonging. In these cases, online social networks can actually enhance users' off-line existence.

Privacy Issues

Regardless of whether social networking technology connects or isolates its users, there is universal agreement that it exposes them to certain risks involving privacy. The information shared between users of online social networks is never really private. After all, the Internet is a public network, the World Wide Web is a public space, and the most popular social networks are open to the public. Once a photograph or a piece of personal data is placed online, it leaves the control of its creator and becomes available to anyone with a computer. Even when users change, remove, or restrict access to the information on their profiles, it can sometimes still be viewed by outsiders with advanced computer skills.

Considering the public nature of social networking sites, computer security experts suggest that users limit the amount

Canada's Privacy Commissioner Jennifer Stoddart holds a news conference on July 16, 2009 to release findings of a report stating that Facebook breaches privacy laws by keeping users personal information indefinitely after members close their accounts.

Cyberbullying: The MySpace Suicide Case

One of the most well-known cases of cyberbullying involves the 2006 suicide of thirteen-year-old MySpace user Megan Meier. Meier killed herself after receiving cruel messages from a fellow MySpace user, whom she believed to be a sixteen-year-old boy named Josh Evans. On the day of her death, Meier received a message from Evans that said, "The world would be a better place without you."

It turned out, however, that Evans does not exist. Lori Drew, the mother of a former friend of Meier, had created a fake MySpace profile in order to gain Meier's trust, obtain personal information, and then humiliate her. Drew wanted revenge against Meier for allegedly spreading rumors about her daughter.

In 2008 Drew was charged with conspiracy and unauthorized use of a computer to inflict emotional distress. Her trial received a great deal of media attention because it was one of the first legal cases to address cyberbullying. A jury found Drew not guilty of conspiracy and guilty on the rest of the charges. A judge later overturned the guilty verdict after concluding that the laws then on the books did not apply to the situation. All the attention surrounding the case led to public calls for tough new laws against online harassment and cyberbullying.

Thirteen-year-old MySpace user Megan Meier killed herself after receiving cruel messages on the site. Her death lead to public outcry to pass tough new laws against online harassment and cyberbullying.

of personal information they make available online. They point out that including such seemingly innocent information as full name, date of birth, and hometown in a profile can enable criminals to obtain a user's Social Security number and steal their identity. Experts also recommend that users avoid filling out questionnaires or taking surveys that are circulated on social networking sites, since they can be used by criminals to gather information.

Even if members of social networks are careful to protect the privacy of their own information, however, they still can be affected by the activities—or security lapses—of distant friends. Sites like Facebook and MySpace, for example, automatically send out updates about each member's activities to everyone on that member's list of friends. Unless a member turns this feature off, it announces when they make a change to their profile, add new friends, and receive messages or comments. If someone posts a suggestive photograph, makes a disparaging remark, or reveals sensitive information on their profile, therefore, it can reach a large number of people instantly.

Such embarrassing material can reflect badly on recipients as well as on the sender. This often creates problems for teenage users of social networks. "What teens post in online public spaces without regard for their privacy and future prospects is the social Web's most common risk for high-school age and college-age people," warn Larry Magid and Anne Collier in *MySpace Unraveled*. "Young people need to think before they post. They need to consider whether they want a prospective employer, for example, to see what they're posting about themselves and their friends."[24]

A growing number of businesses use social networking sites to evaluate potential new employees, and some of these companies acknowledge rejecting some candidates due to objectionable content on their profiles. Such content also can create problems for people after they have joined the workforce. Many people working in a business environment add coworkers to their list of friends on social networking sites, along with friends and relatives. But computer privacy experts recommend keeping work contacts and personal contacts separate in order to maintain a professional appearance with work contacts.

BITS & BYTES

75

Percentage of job recruiters who use Web searches as part of their applicant-screening process

Students also should be aware that the information they post online may not remain private. School administrators and law enforcement officers have increasingly used social networking sites as sources of evidence in disciplinary cases and criminal investigations. In one case, university officials compared students' profile photos on Facebook with pictures of people participating in a violent campus demonstration. Police then used this information to arrest several students. Some legal experts feel that the case raises interesting legal questions about the right to privacy on social networking sites. They assert that these uses of social networks highlight gaps in existing state and federal laws regarding public access to private online content.

Sexual Predators

Although the privacy of social networking profiles is important to all users, children and teenagers are the most vulnerable to the misuse of personal information. Many young people join social networks without fully realizing the risks involved in revealing personal information online. They are often naive about the dangers of interacting with strangers, as well. These factors make it easier for children and teenagers to become the targets of online sexual predators.

In the mid-2000s, the news media was full of sensational stories about sexual predators using social networking sites to locate potential victims. After establishing contact and building trust, often by pretending to be a sympathetic fellow teen, the predators managed to entice their young victims to meet them in person. These real-life encounters frequently ended in sexual assault of the minors. Headlines about such dangerous situations generated widespread fears about Internet safety, as well as intense debate about the use of online social networks by children and teenagers. MySpace, as the most popular social networking site among younger users at that time, became the focus of a great deal of criticism. In fact, concerns about sexual predators prowling the site contributed to the decline in membership that helped Facebook overtake MySpace as the most popular social networking site in the United States.

Despite all the negative publicity, however, instances of Internet-related sexual violence remains rare. "There are only a small number of cases where something bad has actually happened," Internet researcher Danah Boyd notes. "Most of what you are hearing in the press turns out to not be associated with MySpace at all. Just because teens do something stupid/bad and they have a MySpace account does not mean that they did it because of MySpace. Teens are more likely to be abducted at school than on MySpace. Teens are more likely to die in their parents' cars than be killed because of MySpace."[25]

One commonly quoted statistic indicates that one out of every five young people who use the Internet receive an unwanted sexual advance online. The source of this data is the 2000 study *Online Victimization: A Report on the Nation's Youth*. But a closer examination of the results of the study reveals that most of the 19 percent of minors who were sexually solicited online were approached by other minors, rather than by adults. In addition, only 5 percent described the contact as aggressive or said that it made them feel extremely disturbed, upset, or afraid.

Although the risks from online predators may be exaggerated, it is still important for young users of social networking sites to remain alert, think critically, protect their personal information, avoid interacting with strangers, and not arrange to meet a stranger in person.

Social Networking and Personal Information

According to a 2007 study conducted by Cox Communications and the National Center for Missing and Exploited Children, 71 percent of teens ages thirteen to seventeen had personal profiles on social networking sites like Facebook and MySpace. About half the teens surveyed expressed little or no concern about posting personal information online, even though much of the data can be viewed by anyone. The survey shows that teens frequently post the following types of information on social networking sites:

- 64 percent posted photos or videos
- 58 percent posted information about their hometown
- 49 percent posted their school's name
- 8 percent posted their cell phone number

Cyberbullying

While the threat of dangerous strangers lurking on social networking sites has received the most media attention, young Internet users actually face a greater risk of harassment and abuse from their peers. Some of the same mean-spirited behavior that commonly occurs at school also can take place online, including gossip, insults, threats, and sexual harassment. Whether it is perpetrated online or in person, bullying can damage the victim's reputation and self-esteem. But online bullying, commonly known as cyberbullying, sometimes proves even more destructive, because negative information posted on the Internet can spread quickly to hundreds of people.

Cyberbullying can take place on social networking sites, in online chat rooms, or via e-mail, instant messaging, or text messaging. A wide range of behaviors qualify as cyberbullying, including trying to embarrass someone by exposing secret information or circulating compromising photos or videos online; using the Internet to spread malicious rumors or gossip about someone; using profanity, vulgar language, threats, or intimidation in electronic communication; or using technology to impersonate or stalk someone.

Although cyberbullying is sometimes overt and vicious, it also can be careless or inadvertent. Especially among teenagers, there is often a fine line between teasing someone and annoying or embarrassing them. Similarly, what one person considers harmless flirting may appear to another person as sexual harassment. Conversations that might seem innocent when conducted in private can seem much different when they take place in full view of others on a social networking site or in an Internet chat room. Internet security experts encourage parents to remind children and teenagers that forwarding private messages, spreading rumors, and posting sexually suggestive images online is not acceptable and can have serious consequences.

Online safety experts recommend that young people who are troubled by bullies on the Internet confide in a trusted adult. They also suggest that victims of harassment resist the temptation to respond to cyberbullies, and keep copies of

ONLINE EXPERIENCES

About one third (32%) of all teenagers who use the internet say they have been targets of a range of annoying and potentially menacing online activities.

Have you, personally, ever experienced any of the following things online?	Yes	No
Someone taking a private email, IM, or text message you sent them and forwarding it to someone else or posting it where others could see it	15%	85%
Someone spreading a rumor about you online	13%	87%
Someone sending you a threatening or aggressive email, IM, or text message	13%	87%
Someone posting an embarrassing picture of you online without your permission	6%	94%
Answered "yes" to any of the four previous questions	32%	68%

Taken from: Pew Internet & American Life Project Parents and Teens Survey, Oct- Nov. 2006. Based on online teens [n=886]. Margin of error for the overall sample is ±4%, http://www.pewinternet.org/Search.aspx?q=Cyberbullying/ HYPERLINK "http://www.pewinternet.org/~/media/Files/Reports/2007/PIP%20Cyberbullying%20Memo.pdf.pdf" Cyberbullying [K19, PRIV5], accessed on October 30, 2009.

all messages as evidence in case legal action becomes necessary. Incidents of cyberbullying also should be reported to social networking sites, Internet service providers, and local police. Although few laws currently exist to protect people from online harassment, such behavior violates the terms of service for most Web sites and can result in the revocation of a user's privileges.

Children's Safety

A number of resources exist to help children and teenagers use the Internet and social networking sites safely. The Children's Online Privacy Protection Act (COPPA), which took effect in 2000, is a U.S. law that requires all Web sites with content aimed at children age thirteen or younger to obtain parental consent before collecting or using children's personal information. The act also requires such sites to let parents review their children's online profiles. In 2006 the social networking site Xanga was fined $1 million for COPPA violations, such as allowing children to join without verifying their age or obtaining parental consent. Instead of relying on these laws, online safety experts recommend that

Although a number of resources and laws exist to help children use the Internet and social networking sites safely, experts agree that the safest measure is for parents to monitor their children's online activities.

parents take an active role in educating their children about online privacy and safety.

After weighing all the potential problems associated with online social networking, some parents simply decide to prevent their children from using the sites. A number of organizations have reached this conclusion as well. Many schools and public libraries across the United States restrict children's access to the sites. Many businesses, fearing a loss of productivity, block their employees from visiting the sites on company computers. Citing concerns about security, the U.S. Marine Corps banned the use of social networking sites by its personnel in 2009. In addition, a growing number of professional sports teams have prohibited their players from posting messages on Twitter. It remains to be seen whether this trend will affect the overall popularity of social networking in the future.

Tips to Stay Safe Online

The Web site ConnectSafely.com offers the following tips for members of social networking sites to stay safe online:

- Be as anonymous as possible. Consider using a fictitious screen name or a first name only rather than a full name.
- Protect personal information. Avoid giving out identifying details like home address, date of birth, school name, or financial information.
- Think before posting photos. Never publicize anything suggestive or demeaning.
- Avoid in-person meetings. Contacts made on social networking sites may not be who they claim to be.

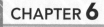

CHAPTER 6

Future Uses and Advancements

Within the space of a decade, online social networks grew from simple, searchable databases of information to dynamic platforms for interactive applications. Facebook, as Steven Johnson writes in *Time*, "went from being a way to scope out the most attractive college freshmen to the Social Operating System of the Internet, supporting a vast ecosystem of new applications created by major media companies, individual hackers, game creators, political groups, and charities."[26] As the networks evolved, their membership expanded from the hundreds into the hundreds of millions. In light of such rapid development and change, many people wonder what direction the technology will take in the future.

Some Internet experts believe that social networking sites will become increasingly open and standardized, enabling users to locate and interact with friends online no matter what tools they use to create their profiles. Other experts predict that social networking services will become increasingly mobile and location aware, allowing users to receive targeted ads and coupons on their cell phone as they walk through a shopping mall, for instance, or to flip through the profiles of nearby patrons at a singles bar. Although many analysts envision online social networking becoming even further ingrained in user's lives, some claim that it will turn out to be a passing fad. "Is it a temporary phenomenon that will crumble under the test of time, or is the concept rife with unlimited potential?" asks Gord Goble in *Digital Trends*. "The answer likely stands somewhere in between."[27]

Increasing Standardization

In the history of online social networking, many different sites have attracted a sudden avalanche of new members and media attention, only to fall from prominence a short time later when an exciting new site appears. When one site replaces another in popularity and media buzz, many people want to follow their friends to the new site.

But social networks like Friendster, MySpace, and Facebook are closed sites or "walled gardens," meaning that they lock in members' personal data and only allow interactions within their centralized systems. These proprietary services do not allow members to export, or transfer, their information to other sites. As a result, people who decide to switch social networks usually must build new profiles, create new lists of friends, and upload new photographs. Many users find this process extremely frustrating and time-consuming. "There comes a point of social networking saturation, where people just don't have the time and energy to join yet one more site, create yet another profile, and make even more friends," explains Mark Glaser of PBS Mediashift. "While social networking sites obviously serve a purpose in helping people connect, there's only so many networks each of us can join."[28]

In response to this problem, some technology experts have promoted increasing standardization and openness in online social networks. Proponents argue that individuals—rather than popular social networking sites—should have the right to control their own online identities, contacts, and content, such as status updates, blog posts, photos, and videos. They want to make it easy for people to take their information with them when they change social networks or share information between multiple social networks.

One possible approach to this challenge involves collecting an individual's information from various social networks and social media sites and combining it in one place. Several entrepreneurs have developed new products, known as aggregating platforms, that are designed to help people organize and access content from different online sources. Jonathan Abrams, founder of Friendster, also was one of the early innovators in the field of aggregating platforms. He introduced a new online service called Socializr that trolls the Internet to find an individual's personal content—such as a profile and contact list on MySpace, photos on Flickr, and blog posts on LiveJournal—and builds a profile that integrates all of the

Friendster Founder Jonathan Abrams

Jonathan Abrams is an Internet entrepreneur who is best known as the creator of Friendster, one of the first successful social networking sites. After earning a bachelor's degree in computer science from McMaster University in Canada, Abrams worked as a software engineer at the Web browser company Netscape for several years. After quitting to try his hand at entrepreneurial ventures, he founded a social bookmarking site called HotLinks that helped people share favorite Web sites with their friends.

Abrams launched Friendster in 2003. The social network grew rapidly, attracting more than 2 million members within six months, and made Abrams one of the most recognizable figures in the world of Internet start-ups. The Web site's management and infrastructure failed to keep pace with its remarkable growth, however, and Friendster soon fell from its position at the forefront of the social networking revolution.

After losing control of Friendster to a venture capital firm in 2006, Abrams turned his attention to other business concerns, such as building a nightclub in San Francisco, California, called Slide. He returned to the Internet business in 2007 by launching Socializr, a Web service that aggregates information from several popular social networking sites to offer people innovative ways to share event and party information with their friends. As of 2009 the site was receiving positive reviews and slowly increasing its user base.

information. Abrams believes that the future of online social networking will favor products that offer users a complete set of features, tools, and experiences. "Now that there are 100 people who have copied my ideas with Friendster, being the 101st social networking site is silly," he says. "I'm building a product that can integrate with those sites."[29]

Creating an Open Social Web

Aggregating information from different social networks is just one approach to overcoming the problems associated with closed, proprietary sites. Another approach, foreseen by many Internet experts, involves doing away with destination sites like Facebook and LinkedIn and turning the World Wide Web into an open, distributed social network. "If we are here in ten years talking about profiles, websites, or social networks, something is really wrong," declares Internet entrepreneur Karl Jacob. Instead, he predicts, "social networks will be woven into every product and thing we touch."[30]

Most experts agree that closed social networking sites will eventually follow the way of Google and become open to everyone.

In 2009 open standards were already available on the Internet that allow individuals to re-create some of the basic services offered by social networking sites. Emerging technologies like OpenID and OpenSocial enable users to insert codes into their online profiles or blog entries to make the content available to many different sites or programs. By standardizing the information, these technologies help people avoid duplication of effort on different sites.

Although using open standards to create a profile requires more effort than simply joining a commercial social networking service, many analysts of future online trends believe that this situation will change. After all, they point out, most users once accessed the Internet through proprietary portals like CompuServe and America Online (AOL). These services eventually gave way to free search sites, like Google, that made the whole Internet accessible to everyone. Many Internet experts consider closed social networking sites to be a throwback to an earlier era and predict that they will follow this long-established pattern of increasing openness on the Internet. "In the long run, open standards usually win," explains Brian McConnell in GigaOM. "The good news for users is that this will be an open market, an ecosystem, with no lock in. Users will be able to choose among many profile and update publishing tools. They'll also be able to use whatever search tool they prefer. Most importantly, users will own their data, and will be able to control how it is presented to the outside world."[31]

Some analysts believe that a company that has already carved out a powerful Internet presence, such as Microsoft, Google, Yahoo!, or AOL, will initiate the move toward open social networking. They predict that one or more of these major players will someday serve as a center for the creation and storage of online identities. Eventually, the continued development of open standards could turn the World Wide Web into an open social network and make conventional closed sites obsolete. Instead of building profiles on different sites, people could have a universal identity online—tied back to a source of personal contact under their control, such as an e-mail address or mobile number—that could be adapted for different purposes. Rather than maintaining a separate list of friends on various sites, people could create a single social graph incorporating all of their contacts.

Opening up online social networks creates a number of interesting new possibilities for interaction. For instance, open social environments could make it easier for people to track the status of their friends in real time. Instead of checking for updates on different social networks, they could use standard feed-reader formats, like those that allow people to receive continuous updates from Twitter or blog sites, to monitor their friends' current activities on the open Web. In addition, new search functions could be developed that relate search terms to an individual's social graph. This type of social search could target results to the individual's needs and interests. If someone searched for news articles on a certain topic, for instance, the search function could emphasize links that had been viewed by that person's friends and colleagues, thus providing avenues for discussion. Similarly,

The DiSo Project

The DiSo Project is an umbrella organization that coordinates efforts to develop new technologies to create an open, decentralized system of social networking on the Internet. DiSo, which is a shortened version of the term *distributed social,* was launched by leading Internet developers Chris Messina and Will Norris in 2007.

The project originated because popular social networking sites like Facebook and MySpace operate as proprietary systems, meaning that they force members to use their platform to interact with other members. Critics describe these sites as "silos" or "walled gardens" because they lock members and their personal data

into centralized systems. Members of Facebook cannot connect with members of MySpace, for example, and people who maintain profiles on both sites cannot share information between them.

To address this problem, the DiSo Project proposes to use open-source software and Web standards to form a decentralized, nonproprietary social network extending across the Internet. Proponents of the project claim that it will give users greater control over their personal information and facilitate the sharing of social data across various Web sites. The DiSo Project is ongoing as of 2009, with a number of prominent members of the Internet community contributing to the effort.

if someone shopped online for a certain product, the search function could refer them to Web sites frequented by people in their social network, thus adding an element of trust and reassurance to their purchasing decisions.

Improving Mobility

As more and more people made online social networking a part of their daily lives, they demanded greater mobile access to the technology. Instead of posting updates and checking for messages only on a home or work computer, users wanted to access their profiles anywhere, at any time, on their Internet-enabled phones or handheld devices. High-tech companies have rushed to put products in the marketplace that can meet these desires, and they have been rewarded with brisk sales that are expected to surge even more in coming years. In fact, according to recent research, the percentage of mobile users who visit online social networks on their phones is expected to increase from 2.3 percent in 2009 to at least 12.5 percent within five years.

Many social networking sites allow members to access their profiles and interact with other members through mobile devices. The main problem facing mobile users is that these devices generally have less memory and processing power than computers, so they are not able to interpret

Experts predict that new applications will be developed to improve mobile access to online social networks such as this Facebook application on this Apple iPod. In the future it may be possible to launch one application and retrieve information from several online communities.

the HTML coding in complex Web pages. As a result, most of the social networking applications available on mobile devices only provide a small subset of the features available online.

Analysts of future Internet trends predict, however, that new applications will be developed to improve mobile access to online social networks. They expect that these applications, like other new developments, will involve increased standardization of information across platforms. In the future, they believe that people will be able to launch a single mobile application and gain access to information from various online communities. "The key is a unified social networking messaging platform that will allow the mobile operator to deliver greater value to their subscribers, empowering them to easily add, remove, and manage their profiles from multiple participating social networking communities within a single application,"[32] notes Jim Knapik in *TechNews-World*. Some analysts also envision the creation of unified mobile address books that will help people store and manage contact lists for phone, e-mail, instant messaging, and other sources in a coherent way.

Although a number of mobile devices already have the capability of GPS technology, computer experts predict that in the future the combination of GPS technology and social networks has the potential to create new uses for these devices.

Integrating Location Awareness

Once social networks become fully accessible through mobile devices, the next technological frontier may involve integrating location awareness with these services. As of 2009, a number of applications used satellite-based Global Positioning System (GPS) technology to track the location of mobile devices. People used products like Google Latitude and foursquare to pinpoint their current position and chart routes to nearby homes, businesses, or attractions.

In the future, however, the combination of GPS technology and social networks has the potential to create a vast array of exciting new uses for mobile devices. People could use their phones to determine the location of all their friends when making plans for a Friday night, or refer to their mobile devices to help them remember the names and occupations of fellow guests at a party or find points of common interest with fellow passengers on a train. Professionals could use the technology to review the qualifications of people speaking at a meeting or conference.

The successful integration of location awareness will depend upon further developments in open standards for online social networking. Michael Arrington explains in *TechCrunch* that further development

> requires a social network that has presence, location, and contextual information about you. . . . It also needs, at a basic level, the ability to sort and browse the people around you based on their picture and name, and what they are looking for (dating, investments, job, friendship). Once this network is established, you'll know everyone's name who's around you (if they choose to share it), and enough basic information to jog your memory if you know them, or meet them if there's mutual interest.[33]

Developing New Uses

Other new uses are likely to appear as online social networks move beyond closed sites and home computers to achieve greater openness and mobility. Business enterprises, for example, may increasingly create social networks to help them connect with employees, customers, and other businesses. Social networks could be crafted into tools to help companies manage their reputations, create brand awareness, generate leads about potential sales prospects, learn about emerging technologies, benchmark against competitors, recruit new employees, gather customer feedback, and improve products and services. The technology also may help small businesses collaborate on large projects or expand their customer base.

Social networks also may gain new applications as an instructional tool in academic and scientific communities. Researchers can use the technology to share information, exchange ideas, and increase knowledge. Colleges and universities can use online social networks to promote courses, communicate with students, conduct group projects, foster peer learning, handle alumni relations, and help students find internship and job opportunities.

The possibilities for online social networking appear endless. Yet some observers remain skeptical about the long-term cultural impact of social networking sites. In fact, there are plenty of people who believe that the technology's phenomenal popularity is likely to fade in the future. Critics claim that reconnecting with old friends and receiving constant updates on their daily activities is a novelty that quickly wears off for many users. They predict that as more people feel the constant intrusion of technology into their daily lives, they will come to appreciate and value connecting with people in old-fashioned, real-world social networks.

NOTES

Introduction: Connecting Online

1. Mike Reid and Christian Gray, "Online Social Networks, Virtual Communities, Enterprises, and Information Professionals—Part 1. Past and Present," Internet Librarian, July–August 2007, www .infotoday.com/searcher/jul07/ Reid_Grey.shtml.

2. TDS Telecommunications Corp., "Internet Service Provider TDS Warns Customers to Think Before Keying Updates on Online Social Network Sites," press release, May 8, 2009, www.prweb.com/ releases/2009/05/prweb2400934 .htm.

Chapter 1 The Internet and Early Online Communities

3. The Well, "Learn About the WELL," The Well, www.well.com/aboutwell .html.

4. Quoted in Anbarasan, Ethirajan, "Tim Berners-Lee: The Web's Brain-child," UNESCO Courier, September 2000, http://www.unesco.org/ courier/2000_09/uk/dires.htm.

Chapter 2 The Development of Online Social Networks

5. Quoted in Max Chafkin, "How to Kill a Great Idea!" Inc., June 2007, p. 84.

6. Gray Miller, "History of Online Social Networking," LoveToKnow Social Networking, http:// socialnetworking.lovetoknow.com/ History_of_Online_Social_ Networking.

7. Brian McConnell, "Social Networks, from the 80s to the 00s," GigaOM, January 20, 2008, http://gigaom .com/2008/01/20/social-networks- from-the-80s-to-the-00s.

8. Chafkin, "How to Kill a Great Idea!" p. 84.

9. Larry Magid and Anne Collier, *MySpace Unraveled: A Parent's Guide to Teen Social Networking*, Berkeley, CA: Peachpit Press, 2007, p. 3.

10. Vanessa Grigoriadis, "Do You Own Facebook? Or Does Facebook Own You?" *New York*, April 5, 2009, www .nymag.com/news/features/55878/ index.html.

11. Grigoriadis, "Do You Own Facebook? Or Does Facebook Own You?"

12. Grigoriadis, "Do You Own Facebook? Or Does Facebook Own You?"
13. Steven Johnson, "How Twitter Will Change the Way We Live," *Time*, June 15, 2009, p. 32.

Chapter 3
How Online Social Networks Work

14. Chafkin, "How to Kill a Great Idea!" p. 84.

Chapter 4
How Online Social Networks Are Used

15. Dan Schawbel, "HOW TO: Build Your Personal Brand on LinkedIn," Mashable: The Social Media Guide, July 27, 2009, http://mashable.com/2009/07/27/linkedin-personal-brand.
16. Quoted in Patrick Patullo, "Yes We Can: Political Campaigns Go Social," Digital Media Buzz, July 14, 2009, www.digitalmediabuzz.com/2009/07/political-campaigns-go-social.
17. Patullo, "Yes We Can."
18. Anastasia Goodstein, *Totally Wired: What Teens and Tweens Are Really Doing Online*, New York: St. Martin's, 2007, p. 152.
19. Deena Guzder, "Facebook Users Go to War over Gaza," *Time*, January 13, 2009, www.time.com/time/world/article/0,8599,1871302,00.html.

20. Quoted in Chris Anderson, "Q&A with Clay Shirky on Twitter and Iran," TED, June 16, 2009, http://blog.ted.com/2009/06/qa_with_clay_sh.php.

Chapter 5
Impact and Implications of the Technology

21. Gord Goble, "The History of Social Networking," Digital Trends, http://news.digitaltrends.com/feature/99/the-history-of-social-networking.
22. Quoted in Ken Grobe, "'Go Talk to a Girl.' Friendster and Socialzr Founder Jonathan Abrams Sets Us Straight on Social Media," *SF Social Media Examiner*, August 10, 2009, www.examiner.com/x-13532-SF-Social-Media-Examiner~y2009m8d10-Go-talk-to-a-girl-Friendster—Socializr-founder-Jonathan-Abrams-sets-us-straight-on-social-media.
23. Quoted in Kevin Hillstrom, *Defining Moments: The Internet Revolution*, Detroit, MI: Omnigraphics, 2005, p. 87.
24. Magid and Collier, *MySpace Unraveled*, p. 3.
25. Quoted in Mark Glaser, "Your Guide to Social Networking Online," PBS, August 29, 2007, www.pbs.org/mediashift/2007/08/your-guide-to-social-networking-online241.html.

Chapter 6
Future Uses
and Advancements

26. Johnson, "How Twitter Will Change the Way We Live," p. 32.

27. Goble, "The History of Social Networking."

28. Glaser, "Your Guide to Social Networking Online."

29. Quoted in Chafkin, "How to Kill a Great Idea!" p. 84.

30. Quoted in Dan Farber, "The Future of Social Networks," ZDNet, August 2, 2007, http://blogs.zdnet .com/BTL/?p=5848.

31. McConnell, "Social Networks, from the 80s to the 00s."

32. Jim Knapik, "Social Networking's Next Frontier: The Mobile Phone," TechNewsWorld, July 30, 2008, www.technewsworld.com/ story/63970.html.

33. Michael Arrington, "I Saw the Future of Social Networking the Other Day," TechCrunch, April 9, 2008, www .techcrunch.com/2008/04/09/i-saw-the-future-of-social-networking-the-other-day.

GLOSSARY

AJAX: Asynchronous JavaScript and XML, a programming language used to create interactive Web applications.

ARPANET: The world's first computer network, developed by the U.S. government's Advanced Research Projects Agency (ARPA) in 1969.

blog: Abbreviation of the word *weblog*, a Web site that serves as an online journal or offers commentary on current events or other topics.

broadband: High-speed Internet connections, including Wi-Fi, cable modems, and digital subscriber lines (DSL).

chat: A real-time, text-based conversation between two or more people using an online chat application or instant-messaging system.

content: A term that encompasses text, pictures, animation, video, and other information on the Internet.

customization: The process of using applications and widgets to change a profile on a social networking site so that it better reflects the user's personal taste and style.

cyberbullying: The use of cruel, offensive, or threatening words or images on the Internet with the intention of embarrassing or harassing another person.

friends: Personal contacts whose profiles are linked to an individual user's profile on a social networking site; also known as buddies, followers, and links.

hypertext: A method for establishing electronic links between text documents using embedded codes or tags created using hypertext markup language (HTML).

packet switching: A method of transmitting data over the Internet that involves breaking information into small pieces called packets, sending the packets across any available connection, and then reassembling them once they reach their destination.

profile: A home page containing personal information that a member provides upon joining a social networking service.

protocol: A basic rule guiding the operation of a computer network, such as transmission control protocol (TCP) and Internet protocol (IP).

really simple syndication (RSS): Software that allows people to syndicate or broadcast regularly updated content, such as news updates, blog posts, or Twitter tweets. Over the Internet; subscribers receive this content using RSS feed readers.

social networking service: A commercial service or Web site that enables users to create personal profiles, establish lists of contacts, share information, and connect with each other online.

URL: Abbreviation for universal or uniform resource locator, the Internet address of a Web site.

widget: A miniapplication or piece of HTML code that can be embedded in a social networking site profile.

World Wide Web: A complex system of software programs and networking protocols that helps people organize and access information on the Internet.

FOR MORE INFORMATION

Book

Terry Burrows, *Blogs, Wikis, MySpace, and More: Everything You Want to Know About Using Web 2.0 but Are Afraid to Ask*. Chicago: Chicago Review Press, 2007. This book explains the basic technology and common usage of a variety of popular Internet social media sites.

Internet Sources

Mark Glaser, "Your Guide to Social Networking Online," PBS, August 29, 2007, www.pbs.org/media-shift/2007/08/your-guide-to-social-networking-online241.html. This article gives the history of online social networks, as well as terminology and resources for readers regarding online networks.

Gord Goble, "The History of Social Networking," Digital Trends, January 21, 2009, http://news.digitaltrends.com/feature/99/the-history-of-social-networking. This article provides readers with the knowledge that social networking is actually older than most people think.

U.S. Federal Trade Commission, "Social Networking Sites," OnGuard Online, September 2007, www.onguardonline.gov/topics/social-networking-sites.aspx. Provides helpful tips for parents and kids regarding the safe use of social networking sites.

Periodicals

Steven Johnson, "How Twitter Will Change the Way We Live," *Time*, June 15, 2009, p. 32.

Web Sites

How Stuff Works (www.howstuffworks.com). This Web site offers explanations of how various things work, written in non-technical language. It provides multiple pages on how to make connections, how Facebook and MySpace works, and points users to more specific networking sites.

PBS (www.pbs.org). PBS is a nonprofit organization offering multipage sections explaining the evolution of online social networking, its advantages and disadvantages to society, and a teacher's section discussing various issues regarding social networks.

INDEX

Internet protocol (IP) (*continued*)
    as part of internetworking protocol, 14
      URL translated into, 39
Internet service providers (ISPs), 36, 37
Internetworking protocol, 14
IP addresses, 37–38
iPods, *80*
Iran, protests against, 60–61
Israel, 59–60

J
Jacob, Karl, 77
JavaScript, 41
Job recruiters, usage by, 67
Johnson, Steven, 74

K
Kahn, Bob, 14
Knapik, Jim, 81

L
LinkedIn, *55*
    creation, 27
    popularity, 27, 44, 54–55
Local-access networks (LANs), 36
Location awareness, 81–82

M
Magid, Larry, 67
Malware, 49
Match.com, 23
McConnell, Brian, 27, 78
Media sharing sites, 35
Meier, Megan, 66, *66*
Membership numbers
    Classmates.com, 23
    Facebook, 30, 31, 75
    Friendster, 26
    LinkedIn, 27, 54–55
    MySpace, 28
Membership process, 42–43, 50–51, 72
Miller, Gray, 26
Mobile social networking
    addiction and, 53–54
    in future, 80–81
    methods and programming language used, 46
    Twitter and, 33
Mosaic, 20
Multimedia messaging services (MMSs), 46
Murdoch, Rupert, 28–29
Music and entertainment sites, 28
MyBarackObama.com, 56–57
MySpace
    cyberbullying on, 66
    development of, 27–28
    Facebook and, 29, 31–32

political protest and, 59–60
popularity, 28–29, 44
sexual predators and, 68–69
as walled garden, 79

N
National Sciences Foundation, 15
Netcom, 17
Network access points (NAPs), 37
Network intersections, 13
News Corporation, 28–29
Nodes, 13
Nonprofit organizations, 59
NSFNet, 14–15

O
Obama, Barack, 56–58
Online safety tips, 73
Online social networks
    changing nature of, 29, 32, 34–35
    most popular, 44
    number among twenty largest Web sites, 12
    number in 2006, 29
    overview of, 10–12
    types, 48–49
Open social networks, 49, 77–80
    See also specific networks such as Facebook
OpenID, 78
OpenSocial, 78
Overuse, 62–65

P
Packet switching, 13
Palestinians, 59–60
Patullo, Patrick, 57
Personal contact, avoiding, 62–65
Phishing, 49
Photos, 46, 52
Point of presence (POP), 37
Political campaigning, 56–58
Political protest, 59–60
Privacy, 44
Privacy issues, 65–68, 69
Profiles. *See* User profiles
Profits, 57
Programming languages
    AJAX, 41–42, *42*
    extensible hypertext markup language
      (XHTML), 46
    See also Hypertext markup language (HTML)
Programs. *See* Applications
Proprietary systems
    aggregating information from, 76–77
    decrease in use of, 78
    examples, 75, 79

PICTURE CREDITS

ABOUT THE AUTHOR

Laurie Collier Hillstrom is a free-lance writer and editor. She is the author of more than twenty books, including *Defining Moments: The Attack on Pearl Harbor* and *People in the News: Al Gore.* She lives in Michigan with her husband, Kevin Hillstrom, and twin daughters, Allison and Lindsay.